GREAT FOUNDERS WRITE

Jimmy,

Thanks for the support.
Happy reading + writing!

Cheers,

Timmy,

Thanks for the support.
Happy reading + writing!

Cheers,

GREAT FOUNDERS WRITE

Principles for Clear Thinking, Confident Writing, and Startup Success

BEN PUTANO

Copyright © 2022 Ben Putano

All rights reserved.

No portion of this book may be reproduced in any form without permission from the publisher, except as permitted by U.S. copyright law. Every effort has been made by the author and publishing house to ensure that the information contained in this book was correct as of press time. The author and publishing house hereby disclaim and do not assume liability for any injury, loss, damage, or disruption caused by errors or omissions, regardless of whether any errors or omissions result from negligence, accident, or any other cause. Readers are encouraged to verify any information contained in this book prior to taking any action on the information.

Published by Damn Gravity Media, Chicago

www.damngravity.com

TABLE OF
CONTENTS

To Mary. I love you most.

WHY GREAT
FOUNDERS WRITE

"Clear thinking is clear writing; one cannot exist without the other."

—WILLIAM ZINSSER

B enjamin Franklin believed true wealth came from hard work and steady progress.

He wasn't just referring to money, but wealth in all forms: happiness, health, personal development, and relationships. He warned his neighbors against risky bets and get-rich-quick schemes. In the last decade of his life, Franklin wrote this in his autobiography:

"Human felicity is produced not so much by great pieces of good fortune that seldom happen, as by little advantages that occur every day."

Franklin put his own advice into practice, day-in and day-out, for eighty-four years. His scope of accomplishments is nothing short of incredible: Franklin was the continent's greatest scientist, inventor, diplomat, business strategist, humorist, and political thinker. He invented bifocal glasses, discovered lightning was electricity, and built the country's first media conglomerate. In politics, he helped unite the embattled colonies and proposed the federal model of government we know today.

"But the most interesting thing that Franklin invented, and continually reinvented," said biographer Walter Isaacson, "was himself."

How did the youngest son of a tradesman become a profitable poet by age twelve, the owner of a print shop by twenty-two, a decorated inventor and scientist in middle age, and a Founding Father in his seventies? No person, not even Franklin, is born with such a broad range of talents. He wasn't a genius in any particular field of study. Instead, Franklin's brilliance was his ability to continually transform himself.

That catalyst for Franklin's transformation through the years? Writing.

"Writing has been of great use to me in the course of my life, and was a principal means of my advancement," he wrote in his autobiography.

Franklin used writing as a tool for personal growth. As a boy, he devised an exercise for himself: he would read a volume of famous essays, set them aside for a few days, and then try to rewrite them from memory. He not only learned how to write like his favorite essayists, but how to think like them.

He also wrote as a means to grow his influence. Throughout his life, Franklin published letters and essays to the public on topics ranging from business and money to politics, civics, health, and war. Some of his letters were written under pseudonyms like Silence Dogood, an old widow, which helped him build empathy for people of all backgrounds. His straightforward and often humorous style won him countless friends and attracted only a few enemies, but even they came around to Franklin eventually.

Franklin wrote to grow his business. When he lacked the funds to start his own newspaper in Philadelphia, he instead wrote for the leading paper in town, *The American Weekly Mercury*. Franklin's goal was to bolster sales of the *Mercury* while tanking the only other paper in the city, *The Pennsylvania Gazette,* thus thinning out the competition. His plan worked. Franklin's essays, which he wrote under the pseudonym Busy-Body, forced a steep decline in sales for the *Gazette*, which Franklin then bought at a discount. He went on to build the most successful media conglomerate of the new world.

Most notably, Franklin used his writing to usher in a new nation. After decades of playing peacekeeper between Britain and the colonies, Franklin became an ardent supporter of American Independence. He wrote the Articles of Confederation—the predecessor to the U.S. Constitution—and played an active role in the Revolution. He even wrote methods and procedures to help General George Washington train the Continental Army. But his greatest contribution to the cause was as an editor. Franklin suggested small but significant changes to Thomas Jefferson's Declaration of Independence. Here's biographer Walter Isaacson again:

> *"[Franklin] crossed out, using the heavy backslashes that he often employed, the last three words of Jefferson's phrase 'We hold these truths to be sacred and undeniable' and changed them to the words now*

enshrined in history: 'We hold these truths to be self-evident.'"

Benjamin Franklin was a great founder in every conceivable way. He founded businesses, clubs, non-profit organizations, schools, political parties, and eventually, a nation. As entrepreneurs, we have so much to learn from his example.

His most enduring lesson? Great founders write.

THE MASTER SKILL

Entrepreneurs are driven. It's in our nature. We're willing to risk our time, money, and reputations to bring our crazy ideas to life. We want to succeed more than anything else in the world—more than sleep, more than comfort, and sometimes even more than our health (though I don't recommend it).

And why are we striving? For independence. Freedom. Wealth. Notoriety. To change the world. To provide a better life for our families for generations to come.

Whether your goal is to build a lifestyle business or the next global giant, you're defined by your drive to succeed. To turn nothing into *something*. To create the world you want to live in.

But all too often, the success you crave stays just out of reach. It's so close you can almost taste it. There seems to be an invisible wall keeping you from your destiny. You'd give anything to reach the other side. What's stopping you?

It's not an invisible wall in your way—it's a mirror.

The thing most often holding us back from entrepreneurial success is ourself. We struggle to share our mission, build support, and empathize with the people we are trying to serve: our customers, shareholders, and teams.

Most importantly, we fail to understand the inner workings of our mind. We stunt our growth with negative thoughts and subconscious habits. We undermine our progress in ways we aren't even aware of.

Yes, there are external barriers to success as well, and some people face more adversity than others. But even external battles are decided by individual actions: your ability to communicate, to rally support, to coordinate global teams, and to paint the vision of a better future for everyone.

These challenges seem numerous and disconnected at first glance. But they all have the same surprisingly simple (though not easy) solution:

Writing.

Writing is the master skill for life and business. It's the most versatile and enduring tool ever invented. And today it's more important than ever—especially for founders.

THE LANGUAGE OF BUSINESS

Writing and entrepreneurship have been linked since the beginning of time—literally.

Historians believe writing was developed for record keeping in ancient Sumer (modern day Iraq). In fact, one of the oldest known pieces of writing, called the Tablet of Kushim, is a business receipt:

"29,086 measures barley 37 months Kushim."

Kushim, the person who signed his name at the end, was not a royal figure or prophet. He was an accountant.

Business has evolved dramatically since the times of Kushim, but the importance of writing has not. If anything, writing has become only more important to the modern entrepreneur.

Thanks to software and the internet, nearly all the traditional barriers to startup entry have been torn down. You no longer need to procure expensive hardware, office space, or even a full-time team. You can build your entire company with on-demand tools and freelance contractors. You can even build a technology company without writing a single line of code.

Anyone can start a company today, and more people are doing just that. Competition is fiercer than ever. You are now competing in a global market, and technology is upending every industry. In the twentieth century, three-to five-year plans were the norm. Today, even twelve-month plans risk becoming obsolete.

The way we work has also changed dramatically. We spend less time in the same room with coworkers. Remote work was already growing in popularity, but the COVID-19 pandemic pushed this fringe trend to the mainstream.

Y Combinator, often considered the world's top startup accelerator, has had a front-row seat to this dramatic shift. Data from their startup-focused jobs platform illustrates the change:

> *"In 2019, just 15 percent of small companies and 10 percent of large companies on the platform were building remote organizations. In 2021, that shifted*

dramatically to 86 percent of small companies and 85 percent of large companies."

What do these massive shifts in entrepreneurship mean for founders? There are three big takeaways:

1. **Writing is now your primary mode of communication**, especially if you lead a remote or hybrid team. Even if your team works in-person, there's a good chance your customers, suppliers, or business partners are dispersed around the globe.

2. **Most companies can no longer compete on logistics, distribution, or even technology.** Instead, messaging is your most reliable competitive edge: what you do, for whom, and why they should care.

3. **You must be more adaptable than ever.** You need the flexibility to change your strategy, build new skills, and lead in new ways. Most importantly, you need to build a deeper understanding of yourself. Writing and journaling are the primary tools for this self-development.

This shift to globalized markets and decentralized work is just the beginning. The future is becoming less predictable. What worked five years ago will not work today, and what works today may not work tomorrow.

Are you ready?

WHAT GREAT FOUNDERS HAVE IN COMMON

Many of the world's most influential entrepreneurs are also prolific writers.

Media mogul Oprah Winfrey has kept a journal since she was fifteen years old. "It's a wonder that I've managed to be a successful human being considering how pathetic I appeared in many of my daily musings," she said in a blog post on her website. "It's a testament to growth and grace that I've come this far."

Jeff Bezos, the founder of Amazon, has built his entire organization on the back of meticulous writing habits. From shareholder letters to product meetings, writing plays an essential role in running the global behemoth (we'll revisit Amazon's writing tactics many times throughout this book).

Tim Ferriss—an entrepreneur, author, and podcast host—credits writing with transforming his life when he was a student at Princeton.

Despite being a neuroscience major, Ferriss took a non-fiction writing course taught by the legendary journalist John McPhee. It was in this class that Ferriss developed the minimalist mindset he's famous for today. Ferriss recalls getting papers back from McPhee where there was more red ink than black. Whole passages were crossed out. "You don't need this," McPhee wrote in the margins.

McPhee didn't just teach Ferris how to write; he taught him how to think. "Once I started taking this writing course, my grades in all of my other classes went up," Ferriss said on his podcast.

And the power of writing extends far beyond business. The world's first two-time Nobel Prize winner, Marie Curie, kept a diary throughout her career, particularly after the death of her husband, who was also her lab partner. She wrote to her late husband as a means to summon the courage to continue their historic work. "I am working in the laboratory all day long, it is all I can do: I am better off there than anywhere else," she wrote.

(A few years later, Curie published a 971-page, Nobel-winning treatise on radioactivity. Talk about prolific.)

The link between writing and personal achievement is undeniable and widely recorded. Just search "benefits of writing" in Google Scholar, and you'll find over 4.1 million results. A paper by Dr. Cecil Smith of Southern Illinois University sums it up best:

> *"Writing enables the external storage of information that can be represented symbolically (e.g., letters, numbers, words, formulas, drawings) and which can then be analyzed, critiqued, reproduced, and transformed, among other potential actions...*
>
> *Writing might be beneficial to cognitive skills because it requires focusing of attention, planning and forethought, organization of one's thinking, and reflective thought, among other abilities—thereby sharpening these skills through practice and reinforcement...*
>
> *Writing is a significant literacy activity in modern life that enables individuals to accomplish a variety of personal, intellectual, occupational, and recreational goals."*

Writing has always been an important skill for entrepreneurs, but it has never been *this* important.

That's why I wrote this book.

THE WRITING BOOK FOR ENTREPRENEURS

Great Founders Write is the book I wish existed when I started my first company. It contains all the lessons I learned the hard way—through the wins and losses of building multiple businesses.

I've worked at the intersection of writing and entrepreneurship for nearly a decade. I'm the founder of Damn Gravity Media, a publishing house for business, creative work, and personal growth books. We partner with founders and business leaders to share their stories with the world. Prior to that I ran WeContent, a content marketing agency for startups and tech companies. We wrote hundreds of pieces that helped our clients grow their audiences.

In preparation for this book, I spent eighteen months studying some of the world's best entrepreneurs, including Sara Blakely, Warren Buffett, Ryan Holiday, Jeff Bezos, and more. I also researched the best work on writing and human psychology from experts like Robert Cialdini, John McPhee, Natalie Goldberg, Stephen King, and William Zinsser.

In addition, I learned from numerous entrepreneurs and writers you may have not yet heard of, but are equally impressive:

- Amanda Natividad, a startup content marketer and trained chef
- Andrew Barry, the founder of a corporate learning development consultancy
- Andy Raskin, a strategic narrative consultant for CEOs and leadership teams
- Arvid Kahl, a developer, entrepreneur, and multi-time author
- Dickie Bush and Nicolas Cole, the founders of Ship30for30
- Drew Eric Whitman, author of *Cashvertising*
- Jay Acunzo, an author, keynote speaker, B2B marketing consultant, and podcast host
- Jamie Russo, author, founder, and former Senior Program Manager at Amazon Advertising
- Josh Bernoff, author of *Writing Without Bullshit*
- Mac Conwell, a multi-time founder and managing partner of Rarebreed Ventures
- Meredith Metzker, a journalist-turned-B2B content marketer
- Shaan Puri, founder and chairman of *The Milk Road*

The result, I hope, is a book that helps every entrepreneur discover (or rediscover) their love for writing.

Great Founders Write is divided into sections based on the four core principles of great writing:

- Write with Purpose
- Write with Empathy
- Write with Clarity
- Write with Courage

It's designed to be practical and immediately applicable. We'll dive deep into specific writing use cases, including marketing, sales, training, persuasion, communication, and more. I'll also show you how to use writing as the ultimate personal development tool.

Finally, you'll find free writing tool like templates, frameworks, and cheat sheets at the end of many chapters. You can access them all by going to **www.greatfounderswrite.com/bonus** and entering your email.

Writing is often considered an art form. This book is not about the art of writing. It's about wielding writing as a tool for your own transformation into a better entrepreneur, leader, and person.

If you're open to the slow, messy, but transformative process of becoming your best self, then this book is for you. Read on.

PART 1
WRITE WITH PURPOSE

"If you don't know where you're going, you might not get there."

—YOGI BERRA

BEGIN WITH THE END IN MIND

How Jeff Bezos Created a Culture of Long-Term Thinking

W hat the *hell* is the point of this?"
We've all read blog posts, landing pages, or long-winded emails that have made us ask this question.

The writing is all over the place. Details are out of order. The writer pummels you with every half-baked thought in their cluttered mind. Worst of all, you don't know *why* you should be reading it in the first place. You eventually (and rightfully) give up. You'll never get that time back and refuse to waste any more.

This, my friends, is a failure to write with purpose.

Writing with purpose means beginning with the end in mind. It's having a clear intention for both yourself and the reader. Few entrepreneurs have demonstrated such clear, purpose-driven writing as Jeff Bezos.

For nearly twenty years, Jeff Bezos, founder and former CEO of Amazon, broke the cardinal rule of publicly traded companies: he didn't prioritize shareholder returns.

Amazon was a public company for nearly five years before it recorded a cent of profit: literally $0.01 per share in the final quarter of 2001. Despite making billions in revenue, it took until 2003—nine years after its founding—for Amazon to post a profitable year. Even then, the company distributed just $0.08 per share, a laughable return compared to competitors like eBay ($0.75 per share), Walmart ($1.81 per share), or Sears ($2.24 per share).

Value investors like Warren Buffett dismissed Amazon as just another internet company doomed to fail like so many did in the early 2000s. In the eyes of skeptics, Amazon would never turn a significant profit. It would eventually shrivel up and go away.

But Bezos proved them all wrong.

How?

By beginning with the end in mind.

Amazon's success is not only a case study in disruptive entrepreneurship, but in purpose-driven writing. Bezos kept investors laser-focused on his long-term strategy: gain market leadership through low prices and exceptional customer service. He reinforced his company's purpose every year in Amazon's shareholder letters.

Unlike Buffett, who was famous for his clear and concise writing, Bezos sometimes rambled in his annual letters. For example, Amazon's 2006 shareholder letter read more like a term paper. Bezos recounted the history of Amazon's database technology and shared minute details of how it all worked. After seven hundred words of tech jargon, Bezos acknowledged, "I'm sure you're wondering why I'm sharing all this." That's when he introduced the next stage of Amazon's AWS business.

Despite his long-windedness, Bezos never let investors forget about Amazon's end goal. They weren't optimizing for short-term profits, but long-term market leadership. He drove this point home by attaching a copy of his first shareholder letter from 1997 to every shareholder letter thereafter.

In that first letter, Bezos outlined the long-term vision of Amazon—not as a bookstore, but as an *everything store*. He made his priorities crystal clear:

It's All About the Long Term

We believe that a fundamental measure of our success will be the shareholder value we create over the long term. This value will be a direct result of our ability to extend and solidify our current market leadership position. The stronger our market leadership, the more powerful our economic model. Market leadership can translate directly to higher revenue, higher profitability, greater capital velocity, and correspondingly stronger returns on invested capital.

Patient investors were eventually rewarded. In Q4 of 2017, Amazon posted $1.86 billion in profit, more than the company made in the previous fourteen years *combined*. In 2021, Amazon's profits soared to over $33 billion—more than Walmart and eBay together. Meanwhile, Sears, once the world's largest retailer, filed for Chapter 11 bankruptcy in 2018.

Bezos is famous for his rallying cry, "Today is still Day 1." It's a reminder to keep building and striving as if you were just getting started. But Bezos was just as focused on his end goal—the grand purpose behind Amazon's strategy.

Whether you're writing a shareholder letter or leading a trillion-dollar company, great founders always begin with the end in mind.

WRITING WITH NO RUDDER

Nothing great is built alone. The best founders are able to rally support around their vision and purpose. They see the future so clearly and vividly, you'd think they've already been there. A powerful *why* is one of the strongest forces behind a successful startup.

But we often forget to identify an equally clear vision and purpose for our writing. We start writing without really knowing what we're trying to say. And once we *do* find the point, we don't edit our work to make it clear. The reader has to slog through lines of rambling just to understand *why* you wrote them in the first place. It's exhausting.

Writing this way is like trying to sail a boat with no rudder. Getting to your intended destination is all but impossible, especially in choppy waters. This isn't just an inconvenience for your reader—it costs your company precious time and actual money.

Josh Bernoff, author of the excellent book *Writing Without Bullshit*, calculated that poor writing costs American businesses $396 billion *every year*.

In his survey of workers who write as part of their jobs,

Bernoff identified the main concerns they have with bad writing:

1. Too long
2. Poorly organized
3. Unclear
4. Too much jargon
5. Not precise enough
6. Not direct enough

These bad writing habits all have the same root cause: writing without a clear purpose.

When we don't know what to say, we ramble. Our ideas are all over the place. We speak in vague terms instead of specific details. We use big words to cover up our lack of understanding. We don't give precise or clear directions. We use phrases like, "What I'm trying to say is..." or "Long story short..." as if this makes up for wasting our reader's time.

Better writing begins with the end in mind.

And there's just one question you need to ask yourself to get started.

WHY ARE YOU WRITING THIS?

With any powerful tool, careful aim is vitally important. Writing is no different.

Bezos has a clear purpose for every shareholder letter: to reinforce Amazon's long-term mission of market leadership. Most of the time, your purpose is more mundane, like rescheduling a meeting. Big or small, you need to know what you're trying to achieve.

Start every piece of writing by asking yourself, "Why am I writing this?" It doesn't matter if it's an email or a book. In fact, the shorter the communication, the more important the question.

I often write, "Why am I writing this?" at the top of my doc or email before drafting. When I hit a writer's block, it's usually because I have forgotten the purpose of the piece, and I ask myself the question again.

Here are other useful variations of the question:

- What am I really trying to say here?
- What action do I want my reader to take?
- What am I trying to achieve?
- What emotion do I want my reader to feel?
- If my reader only remembered one thing, what do I need it to be?

You can also find the purpose of your writing through freewriting. Just start writing to see where it goes. When I do this, I typically find my real purpose somewhere in the middle of my ramblings. (I share a specific freewriting exercise in Chapter 15).

But here's where most founders go wrong: they fail to edit their first draft or publish it as is. (We'll discuss editing in more detail in Section 3, Writing with Clarity.) Your reader should know the purpose of your writing at the *beginning* of your work, not the middle or the end. The burden of understanding is always on the *writer*.

Writing with purpose isn't complicated, but it does take a few deliberate moments of thought before you share your work with others. For your readers, it will be considered time well spent.

DEFINING A POWERFUL PURPOSE: WRITE LIKE A DEVELOPER

Sometimes you need your writing to resonate on a deeper level. You aren't just firing off an email, but trying to convince a superstar designer to join your team. Or maybe you're creating the landing page for a brand-new product that has the potential to triple your business.

When you need to define a deep, emotional purpose for your writing, don't turn to visionary founders for inspiration. Talk to your software development team.

Software developers and product managers are masters of purpose-driven writing. They do it every day. You won't find their work in Google Docs or on your blog, but in your task management system.

I'm talking about product user stories.

Before building a new feature, developers and product managers must explain *why* the feature should exist. User stories define a feature's *purpose*, not just its function. Not doing this could cost hundreds of thousands, if not millions of dollars, in wasted effort.

Here's the standard template for a product user story:

> *As a [specific user], I want to [action] so that [definition of success] + [emotional and rational benefits].*

For example:

> *As a **shift manager** [user], I want to **see the time-off requests of all my employees at a glance** [action] so that **I can quickly create next week's work schedule***

> *[success]* **without the stress and frustration of flipping back-and-forth between emails** *[benefits]*.

Notice what the user story *doesn't* include: a description of the new feature. That's because product managers (who often write the user stories) don't want to prescribe what the engineers should build. Their job is to share the *purpose* of the project and let the developers come up with the best solution.

Product user stories teach us four rules about defining a powerful purpose:

1. Address a *specific person*, not the general public.
2. Focus on the person's *actions*, not the features they'll use.
3. Share a clear definition of *success*.
4. Describe *emotional* as well as *rational* benefits.

Remember: When you ask yourself, "Why am I writing this?" don't just answer rationally. Search for an emotional reason why the reader should care.

You can use this user story template in all forms of writing. Let's say you're trying to recruit that superstar designer to your team. Your first answer to "Why am I writing this?" might be this:

Convince Chris Do to join our team as head of product design.

That's *just ok*, but probably not enough to convince a world-class designer like Chris Do to join your team (you'll learn more from Chris in Chapter 12). You need a more powerful purpose.

Let's use the product user story template and try again

(we'll switch the template to your perspective instead of the user's perspective):

> *Why am I writing this?*
>
> *Chris Do [**user**] will join our team as head of product design [**action**] so that he can design products that not only matter, but are wildly successful [**success**]. He will have the autonomy and support of a world-class team to bring his vision to life [**emotional benefit**] and could also earn significant upside in the business [**rational benefit**].*

- Specific user: Chris Do
- Action: Join team as head of product design
- Success: Design products that not only matter, but are wildly successful
- Emotional benefit: Autonomy and world-class team to bring vision to life
- Rational benefit: Earn significant upside in the business

When developing your powerful purpose, details matter. Get specific with your reader's actions, benefits, and definition of success. Spend more time than you think you need to define your purpose. Then watch your writing flow with energy and focus.

Founders write for many purposes, each of which requires a different approach. Let's look at three: writing to inform, writing to sell, and writing to teach and train.

$$2$$

SAY THE MOST IMPORTANT THING FIRST

How to Improve Your Daily Communication

L et's talk about the most common form of writing in your work today: email.

It's easy to take emails for granted. They're so routine that we don't even think about them as writing. They're just busywork—something we *do*. But because emails are so ubiquitous, small improvements in the way we write them can make a massive difference over time.

Think about these three email subject lines. What do they have in common?

Subject: *Updated health insurance policy*

Subject: *All-hands meeting this afternoon—urgent*

Subject: *We're being acquired*

Not much, right? Number one is pretty mundane, number two seems to imply an existential crisis, and the last one is exhilarating or terrifying, depending on your equity package.

But the fundamental purpose of each email is the same: to inform the reader of something important.

The vast majority of our writing as founders is basic communication. The sharing of information. It's always been this way, dating all the way back to the invention of writing as a record-keeping system. But today, sharing information is almost *too* easy, and this has made our writing sloppy. Emails are often disorganized and full of unnecessary details, and they fail to answer our reader's most pressing question: "What does this information mean *for me*?"

The internet has given us infinite space to write, but now we're constrained by an even more limited resource: our reader's attention span.

When writing to inform, being organized is critical. You need to lead with the most important information and leave zero ambiguity about what it means. Cut any extraneous information or save it until the end. This is not the time to lead with an "interesting" backstory or wax poetically about your company's mission.

Never forget the cardinal rule when writing to inform: get to the point.

Here's a real example of an internal email that plagues thousands of businesses around the world (names have been changed to protect the guilty):

Subject: Product meeting

Hi all,

Been a wild day. Andrew from XYZ Ventures just put a meeting on my calendar for this afternoon. I'll need the pitch deck updated by 2 so I have time to review and rehearse a bit. Obviously the product meeting is a blocker now. Let me know what you'd like to do.

-B

—

Boss McFounder

"Be the change you wish to see in the world."

Imagine you're the Head of Product for this company. Do you know what to make of this email? What does Boss McFounder want you to do, exactly? Should you change the meeting time or have it without him? And why is he telling you about the pitch deck? You're not responsible for that.

It's obvious this founder did not consider the purpose of his email. Instead of organizing his thoughts, he wrote it as a pure stream-of-consciousness, leaving everyone confused and unsure what to do next.

How would you fix this message?

THE INVERTED BUSINESS PYRAMID

We can learn a lot about informational writing from our friends in the news media. Their job is to share information (ideally) without judgment or bias.

To do this, they use a time-tested writing framework called the *inverted pyramid*.

Inverted Pyramid (Journalism)

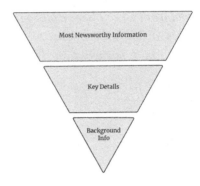

The *inverted pyramid* prioritizes the most important information at the top, followed by key details, and ends with background information. Journalists adopted this framework for two reasons. First, it respected the reader's time by sharing the most newsworthy information up front. Second, in the age of physical newspapers, it ensured no critical details were lopped off the end to make room on the page.

Founders have their own inverted pyramid when writing to inform:

The Inverted Business Pyramid:

1. Purpose (i.e., most important thing)
2. Key details
3. What does this mean for the reader?
4. Background info (if needed)
5. Next steps

The Inverted Business Pyramid

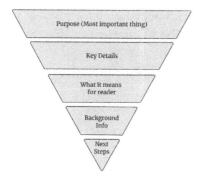

Let's rewrite Boss's email using the inverted business pyramid:

> *Subject: Rescheduling product meeting*
>
> *Hi all,*
>
> *I'll need to reschedule our product meeting. I just had an investor call pop up on my calendar. Does 4 pm work for everyone instead? If so, please send over an updated calendar invite. Thank you.*
>
> *-B*
>
> ―
>
> *Boss McFounder*
>
> *"Clarity is kind" –Brené Brown*

Here's the breakdown:

- **Purpose:** Rescheduling the product meeting.
- **Key details:** An investor call has interrupted the original plans.
- **What it means for the reader:** They'll have to adjust their schedule for the 4pm meeting or suggest a different time.
- **Background info:** None. The Head of Product is likely aware that the company is trying to raise money. This call is important.
- **Next steps:** Send a new invite to Boss.

Boss McFounder leaves no ambiguity in his new message. It has a clear purpose, clear consequences for those involved, and clear next steps. This is the type of email that can save your business hundreds of hours over the years.

Here's another example of the inverted business pyramid in action, this time in a longer piece of writing: Jeff Bezos's announcement that he was stepping down as CEO of Amazon.

(I'll just share the relevant sections here, but I highly recommend you read the entire letter):

Purpose (First sentence):

Fellow Amazonians:

I'm excited to announce that this Q3 I'll transition to Executive Chair of the Amazon Board and Andy Jassy will become CEO.

Key details (second sentence):

In the Exec Chair role, I intend to focus my energies and attention on new products and early initiatives.

What this means for the reader (third sentence):

Andy is well known inside the company and has been at Amazon almost as long as I have. He will be an outstanding leader, and he has my full confidence.

[In other words, you have nothing to worry about.]

The body of Bezos's letter is a reflection on his time as the CEO of Amazon. It's a great story, but not mission-critical for the reader.

Next steps (final paragraph):

Keep inventing, and don't despair when at first the idea looks crazy. Remember to wander. Let curiosity be your compass. It remains Day 1.

The formatting of Bezos's letter was not an accident. Jamie Russo, author of *The Underdog Paradox* and a former Senior Program Manager at Amazon Advertising, shared with me a core writing principle he learned from his time at the company:

BLUF, or Bottom Line Up-Front.

BLUF originated in the U.S. military to simplify communications. Now it's used to guide every piece of writing within Amazon. "The idea is to put the most important details first. People are busy," said Russo. "BLUF saves everyone time and makes the point clear."

Bezos's letter is a masterclass in the BLUF principle. Notice how he hits the purpose, key details, and what they mean for the reader in the first three sentences. He wastes no time getting to the point.

When writing to inform, act like your space is limited—because it is. Not by the dimensions of your piece of paper, but the attention span of your reader. Follow the inverted business pyramid to get to the point fast.

But not all of your writing is simply designed to share information. As a founder, your most important job is to *sell*.

That's next.

FREE TOOL #1 BONUS:
Inverted Business Pyramid Template

Purpose-driven writing will improve your daily communication immediately.

Go to **www.greatfounderswrite.com/bonus**, enter your email, then click on "Inverted Business Pyramid" to get the free template. Use this tool any time you need to share important information with your team or customers.

SELL WITH STORYTELLING

How to Write Convincing Copy for Your Startup

Copywriting is sales at scale.
One great piece of writing can do the job of a thousand salespeople. Strong copywriting will improve every aspect of your business, from your website to sales emails to paid ads and job descriptions. It's one of the most powerful skills you can learn as a founder.

But copywriting is especially hard for startups because *no one knows who you are.* Big companies have established customer bases who know, like, and trust them. They offer proven solutions to known problems. Startups often start at square one: convincing potential customers they have a problem worth solving. Even if the problem is well known, you have to convince customers to ditch their current solution and take a chance on you. Either way, it's an uphill battle

As a general rule, people hate change. So how do you convince someone your product or service is worth the effort to switch? How do you build trust, sell your solution, and generate demand in just eight seconds—the average attention span of someone on the internet?

Master copywriters don't start every new project from scratch. They use proven copywriting frameworks to press all the right psychological buttons, every time. But most frameworks, like PAS—Pain, Agitate, Solution—were created for big companies. They work wonderfully when you have a well-known brand. Startups need their own copywriting framework.

It's time to learn your ABC123s.

COPYWRITING FOR STARTUPS: ABC123

The best copywriting combines sales and storytelling.

This is especially true for startups. You need to convince customers the world is changing around them, then present a new path to a more beautiful future. Along the way, you must build enough trust and urgency to trigger the action you want them to take.

While running WeContent, my content marketing agency for startups, I struggled to fit our clients' narratives into traditional copywriting frameworks. So my team and I set out to create something new: a copywriting framework that positioned startups as the *obvious* solution to an *urgent* problem in their customers' lives.

After two years of trial and error, I developed the ABC123 framework:

A - **ATTENTION**

B - **BIG** change or idea

C - "Why should I **CARE?**"

1 - **SOLUTION**

2 - "Why **YOU?**"

3 - **URGENCY**

The ABC123 framework is designed to be as flexible as it is powerful. Each step addresses a key psychological need of a potential new customer. Use this tool to write landing pages, product descriptions, sales emails, paid ads, social media posts, video scripts, and even job descriptions (another form of sales).

Let's explore each step to learn what it is, why it works, and how to use it to generate sales.

A – Attention

The first job of copywriting is to grab your customer's attention: their most valuable and finite resource. This is much easier said than done. We're producing more content than ever; on Twitter alone, 500 million posts are published every day.

So how do you stand out in such a noisy world?

There are three proven ways to earn your customer's attention:

- Be specific
- Create F.O.N.K.
- Evoke emotion

Be specific

In a stadium full of 50,000 screaming fans, with Darius Rucker playing on the largest stage I've ever seen, one single voice caught my attention.

"Hey, Ben!"

It was my brother coming back from the concession stand, arms full of snacks and drinks. I grabbed the popcorn from him and got back to singing along with Darius.

How could I hear my brother's voice in the crowd? Because he used my name. Specificity cuts through the noise.

According to pioneering psychologist D.E. Broadbent, human brains apply a filtering strategy for managing stimuli. We simply can't process everything, so we only process the things that matter to us. Broadbent's Filter Model of Attention explains why you notice every Jeep Wrangler on the road as soon as you buy one yourself (or even think about buying one). It's also why I could hear my name called out in a massive crowd.

You can use your customer's selective attention to your advantage. The key is to be specific. Use your customer's specific job title in your landing page headline. For example, Damn Gravity's current home page headline reads, "The Book Publisher for Entrepreneurs." I grab the attention of any entrepreneur interested in writing a book. That's the goal.

Here are more ways to be specific:

- Personalize emails using your customer's name or company.
- When comparing your product to your competitors, call them out by name.

- Use memes or inside jokes only your customers will understand.
- Make your pain points ultra specific .
- Use language your customers would use. Don't say "Acquire a new account" when your customers say "Close the deal."

Specificity must be well-aimed, otherwise you'll just blend in with the noise. The better you know your customer, the more specific—and effective—your copy will become.

Create F.O.N.K.

Grab your customer's attention by posing a question they simply *must* learn the answer to.

This is creating F.O.N.K., or the Fear of Not Knowing. Like its cousin, F.O.M.O. (Fear of Missing Out), it's a very real phenomenon. In fact, F.O.N.K. helped an unknown business teacher write one of the best-selling business books of all time:

How to Win Friends and Influence People by Dale Carnegie.

The book's title wasn't written by Carnegie himself, but a young copywriter named Victor Schwab. (Schwab would later be named The Greatest Mail Order Copywriter of All Time by *AdAge*.) It's the epitome of generating F.O.N.K. and has inspired countless copycats. *How to Win Friends* sold over one million copies in its first three years, shattering records and kickstarting the self-help book genre.

To create F.O.N.K., you need to ask a question your

customers deeply care about. Carnegie's book wouldn't have sold as well if it was titled *How to Have Better Conversations*. Sure, that's what the book is about, but readers cared about the *benefits* of better conversation: winning friends and influencing people.

(We'll dive deeper into the question of making your customers care later on in this section.)

Evoke emotion

Shaan Puri, co-founder of *The Hustle* and creator of the Power Writing course, starts each piece of writing by deciding which emotion he wants to evoke in his readers. Here's his reference list:

LOL: That's hilarious!

WTF : This pisses me off

AWW: So cute!

WOW: That's unbelievable!

NSFW: Woah... That's crazy.

OHH: I finally get it! That always confused me.

FINALLY: Someone said what I've been feeling!

YAY: That's great news!

Emotion is a powerful attention-grabber. Unfortunately, negative emotions are more potent than positive ones. For example, one of Puri's best-performing Twitter threads starts like this:

So... everyone seems to think clubhouse is the "next big thing"—but I think it's going to fail.

Here's how I think it all goes down...

At the time, Clubhouse was the fastest-growing social media platform in the United States and had created a cult-like following. His take pissed a lot of people off (WTF!), but it piqued their curiosity as well. Maybe Puri knew something about Clubhouse they didn't (in other words, he created F.O.N.K.).

Evoking emotion has its pros and cons. On the one hand, it's extremely effective. On the other, some people avoid brands that poke the bear too often. Don't be extreme for its own sake unless stoking controversy is part of your brand.

If trying to gain attention makes you feel dirty, you're not alone. No one wants to add to the clickbait pandemic. But remember this piece of advice from Ship30for30 co-founder Dickie Bush: "It's only clickbait to fail to deliver on your promise."

Bush's co-founder, Nicolas Cole, went even further: "If you have valuable information to share with people, it's your obligation to package it in a way that grabs them."

So if you really believe in your business, it's your duty to get your customer's attention—just be sure to deliver on your promise.

B – BIG Change

"An object at rest stays at rest."
Newton's first law of motion applies to more than just

physics. It describes customer behavior as well. Most people won't act unless something forces them to. Your job is to shake them from their comfortable status quo. You need to introduce a BIG change.

What big changes are happening in your customer's world? These could be internal or external changes—ideally, you have both. Are they getting married? Did their doctor scare them into eating healthier? Did the government introduce a new tax credit that could save their company millions? Is their industry on the verge of technological disruption?

Below is an example of a BIG change from Zuora, a subscription management software company. Andy Raskin, the king of corporate strategic narratives, made this example famous in his viral *Medium* post "The Greatest Sales Deck I've Ever Seen."

Here's Raskin:

> *"Don't kick off a sales presentation by talking about your product, your headquarters location, your investors, your clients, or anything about yourself.*
>
> *Instead, name the undeniable shift in the world that creates both (a) big stakes and (b) huge urgency for your prospect.*
>
> *The first slide of virtually every Zuora deck—sales or otherwise—is some version of this: 'We Now Live in a Subscription Economy.'"*

Every decision has a cost, and it's not just the price of your product or service. Switching costs—or the time and effort that go into making a change—can be overwhelming. The BIG change in your customer's world must be significant enough to make those switching costs worthwhile.

Sometimes the problem isn't a big change in your customer's world, but *a lack of change*. Stagnant industries are the perfect place to introduce your disruptive new product or service. In these cases—such as the world of book publishing where I reside—your job is to convince potential customers that big change *needs* to happen. Why? Because their livelihoods depend on it. Focus on what your customer is *losing* by doing nothing, then paint a picture of the opportunities available to them if they embrace change.

In the publishing world, we need a revolution. Traditional publishers leave authors high and dry, while self-publishing is still difficult and time-consuming. Authors deserve a better option: performance publishing (this is the *Solution*, which we'll get to soon).

But you can't just claim the sky is falling. You have to prove big change is happening (or needs to happen) with both statistics and anecdotes (sales and storytelling). Show your customers the change is *real* and it's happening *now*.

Then you must convince them to *care*.

C – "Why should I CARE?"

In a world screaming for our energy and attention, nothing is harder than getting someone to care about what you're building. Never assume the benefits of your product or service are self-evident—you must explicitly answer your customer's most pressing question:

"Why should I care?"

Generally speaking, humans care about four things: health, wealth, time, and happiness. There are infinite nuances here, but most of our motivations fall into one of these buckets. (We'll go deeper into the subject of human motivation in Chapter 6.)

In addition, reams of psychological research have proven that humans care more about *losing* things than gaining them. Studies conducted by Nobel-winning behavioral economist Daniel Kahneman found that losing $100 was just as motivating as *winning $200*. In other words, we care twice as much about losing something as we do about gaining it.

So when answering the question, "Why should I care?" don't just tell your customer what they'll gain; show them what they'll *lose* if they don't act now.

Loss-aversion copywriting is a tough balance. You don't want to come off like a fearmonger. One trick to avoid this is to pair every loss statement with a gain statement. Here's an example from my friend Justin Moore's Twitter bio—in my opinion, a masterstroke in copywriting:

> *"I teach you how to find & negotiate your **dream sponsorships** so that you can **stop leaving money on the table**." (Emphasis mine)*

Justin perfectly captures what customers will gain by working with him (dream sponsorships) and what they could lose if they don't (money on the table).

When doing research for your copy, make two lists: What customers will gain if they work with you, and what they will lose if they don't. Then experiment with different pairings to create the most powerful answer to the most important question:

"Why should I care?"

1 – Solution

You've now grabbed your customer's attention, showed them a big change happening in their world, and convinced them to care and act.

Here's where you strike: present your product or service as the *obvious* solution for your customer's *urgent* problem (more on urgency later). You know exactly what your customer needs to take advantage of the big change—to help them maximize their gains and minimize their losses.

This is the part of the copy where you stop talking about your customer's world and focus on your product or service. When presenting your solution, you need to be detailed enough to answer your customer's technical questions, but not so thorough that you lose their interest.

If you've heard any piece of copywriting advice in the past, it was probably this: "Talk about the benefits of your product, not the features." This is only half correct.

Think about a time when you landed on a company's website. It was well designed with compelling copy and cool visuals. But after reading it, you still had *no idea* what the company actually did. This is a huge problem, especially for startups.

Here's a real example of a B2B SaaS company's website (name omitted to protect the guilty):

Title: Be your customer's shipping hero

Subtitle: Smarter logistics for a faster world—without the hassle

Benefit 1: Fast, simple, smart

Always deliver when you say you will—without the pain of constant maintenance.

Benefit 2: Ready to scale with you

Don't worry about switching tools as you grow. We're here for you every step of the way.

Benefit 3: Your partner in shipping

You'll deal with humans, not chatbots. 24/7 support when your customers need it.

Based on this website copy, do you really know what this company does? I don't. The benefit statements are compelling, but as a potential customer, I'm not going to waste my precious time trying to decipher what they do.

The fix is simple: when presenting your solution, share both benefits and features. Benefit/feature pairings will help customers connect your solution to their problem. Be very clear when describing your features. To quote an anonymous genius, "Confused customers don't buy."

Let's update the copy above to clarify the features:

Title: Be your customer's shipping hero

Subtitle: Third-Party logistics—without the hassle—for fast-growing retailers

Benefit 1: Fast, simple, smart

Get up-to-the-minute shipping recommendations with our AI-powered logistics engine so you always deliver when you say you will.

Benefit 2: Ready to scale with you

Don't worry about switching tools as you grow. Pricing based on shipping volume, not a subscription, so you only pay for what you need.

Benefit 3: Your partner in shipping

24/7 support when you need us. Send customer support inquiries directly to us, where your customers talk with humans, not chatbots.

You've done the hard work of making your customer care. Don't waste their time by not clearly describing what you do. Share both benefits *and* features.

2 – "Why YOU?"

But even the most convincing pitch won't inspire people to act if they don't know you or trust you.

This is the highest hurdle for startups to clear. Without an established track record, how do you convince potential customers to take a chance on you?

The question of "Why you?" has a three-part answer: your mission, expertise, and social proof.

Mission

Why did you start your business in the first place? If it was just to make a quick buck, you'll have a hard time getting customers to trust you. Customers want to know you're in this for the long haul. They need to know you care deeply about the business, and by extension, your customers.

Expertise

Your company may be new, but what's your personal experience in the industry? Why are you an expert in this field? If you aren't an expert, don't pretend to be. Instead, borrow expertise from business partners, co-founders, or advisors.

Social proof

Finally, are you trustworthy? Will other people vouch for you? It's critical to secure early testimonials or reviews any way you can (besides faking them, of course.) If you're struggling to attract those first few customers, offer to do work pro bono. Then do a fantastic job and ask for a testimonial. Even a single piece of social proof is enough to get off the ground.

Finally, when you're just starting out, it helps to offer some sort of guarantee:

- Satisfaction or your money back
- 30-day risk-free trial
- No credit card needed
- No contract—cancel anytime

Remove any risk from choosing you. Customers need to know they can safely abandon ship if you start to sink.

3 – Urgency

The last piece of great copywriting is urgency. Why should your customer act *right now*?

Creating urgency is a delicate balance. You want to press your customer without being pushy. Ideally, as Andy Raskin pointed out, your BIG change should generate huge urgency on its own. But you can also add layers of urgency to create an offer customers can't refuse.

There are three tools at your disposal to create urgency: scarcity, action-oriented language, and no-brainer offers.

Scarcity

If you have limited capacity to serve customers, you can use scarcity to create a sense of urgency. This includes limited-time offers, finite seats available, or one-of-a-kind products like NFTs. Scarcity is the most powerful tool for generating urgency, but don't overuse it. If the customer catches a whiff of dishonesty, like if you're artificially limiting supply, you'll lose their trust and likely lose them as a customer.

Action-oriented language

When writing your calls-to-action, use descriptive verbs to promote urgency. For example, compare these two CTAs for setting up a demo:

- Request a demo
- See it in action

Which button would you be more likely to click? "See it in Action" promises an immediate payoff, while "Request a demo" is vague and a little intimidating. Inspire action by making the next step crystal-clear.

No-brainer offer

When in doubt, make your offer so good customers would feel dumb not taking you up on it. Casper's 100-day trial set a new standard in the mattress industry. It was such a stupidly good offer that customers had no reason *not* to try it.

Another way to make your offer a no-brainer is to make it insanely easy to sign up. Use integrations like Google Sign-In or Apple ID to make the sign-up process as fast as possible. This will encourage customers to just sign up immediately instead of waiting.

Practice Makes Perfect

There's no right way or wrong way to write copy.

For every "rule," there is an example of a wildly successful campaign that breaks it. The only true test of great copy is this—does it work? And the only way to answer that question is through trial and error.

Feedback is the real secret ingredient of great copywriting. The more you can get, the better your copy will be. This is why I love social media platforms like Twitter for quickly sharing ideas and getting feedback. Test your copy in a Tweet to see if you're getting the attention and reaction you want. Don't have a large enough following? You can always cold email or direct message potential customers and get instant feedback. Even no response is feedback—figure out a different way to get a reaction.

And remember: great copy will get customers through the door, but deliver on your promises to keep them around.

FREE TOOL #2 BONUS:
ABC123 Framework Template

Use the ABC123 framework to tell your story and land more customers.

Go to **www.greatfounderswrite.com/bonus**, enter your email, then click on "ABC123 Framework" to get the free template. Use this framework to write copy for your landing pages, sales emails, paid ads, or content marketing.

(4)

TRAIN YOUR TEAM
FOR SUCCESS

*How to Build Teaching Material to Scale
Your Company the Right Way*

I wish I had known Andrew Barry back in 2018. He would have saved me a lot of pain... and money.

Instead, I had to learn the hard way what happens when a fast-growing company fails to properly train their team.

WeContent was finally picking up steam. After months of cold outreach, I had just closed our best month ever—literally double the revenue from the month prior. But that also meant we had twice as many blog posts to write. I quickly got to work contracting three new writers and a freelance editor to meet the demand. The folks I found had good resumes and strong portfolios. I assigned them to my existing accounts so I could focus on our new, bigger clients.

Companies hired WeContent to teach complex tech topics through blog posts and white papers. The irony is that when I hired my new teammates, I failed to teach them the process that had made us successful. Instead of taking the time to train my team, I simply assigned article topics and deadlines for the first drafts.

The writers submitted their work promptly, but I was too busy for a proper review. After a quick scan of each piece, I sent the first batch of articles over to my longest-standing client. About a day later, I got this email from the CEO:

Ben -

First, I'll say the first 10 or so articles are absolutely amazing and have been really good for us, have gotten a lot of great feedback. You knocked it out of the park.

That said, wanted to drop you a line as I would want someone to tell me. ***The quality has dropped off significantly.***

Totally understand this might be a part of the leveling up process but I'll just say the last few articles we've gotten back have been pretty rough. I think Laura can give some more detailed feedback as well but what I'm seeing is:

- I've spent more time editing these last 3 or 4 articles than all other articles combined, that's not taking into account Laura's time.

- **The lack of understanding of our product, platform and general company is frustrating**
- Our voice from the first several articles is completely gone. Zero conversational tone. **These feel worse than reading a research paper.**

Let me know how we can improve on our side to get you what you need.

(Emphasis mine)

By the time I got that email, it was too late. I had commissioned about 30 blog posts for that month, and all of them were coming back with the same issues in quality, research, and voice. I had no choice but to pay the contractors (it wasn't their fault), let them go (I couldn't afford to pay them again), and rewrite all the articles myself. It took me three months to catch up, during which I received no pay and lost half of my new clients.

That takes us back to Andrew Barry. Had I known him in 2018, I would have learned the critical lesson of training my team for success.

Barry is an accountant by schooling but a teacher by passion. After working in corporate training for a decade, he started a learning development and consulting group called Curious Lion. Barry has worked with organizations ranging from Pinterest to KPMG to the NBA.

Curious Lion does more than build online training programs—they create learning cultures within companies. When education becomes a habit, you're able to grow your business without the false starts like we had at WeContent.

Much of your job as a founder is to teach and train. You have to teach potential customers about your unique approach and solution (See Chapter 3: Sell With Storytelling). You also need to train employees, contractors, and virtual assistants to run the ship while you continue steering. Fail at one of these jobs and you'll run out of fuel. Fail at the other, and you'll blow up the engine.

But teaching is more than just the transfer of information. Facts and formulas are useless without knowing why they're important, where they fit into the big picture, and how to use them.

Almost all of your training material will be in written form (even training videos start out as scripts.) So what does good training content look like?

To set your team up for success, let's look at Andrew Barry's 5-Step Framework for writing training material:

1. Building blocks
2. Key learning outcomes
3. Delivery format
4. Storyboard
5. Reinforcement

1. BUILDING BLOCKS

Before you write a single step of your training program, let's go over the fundamentals. We'll call these *building blocks* because they set the foundation for your program. Your building blocks include resources, principles, and your employees' levels of prior knowledge.

Resources

Your resources are the content, tools, and experts at your disposal.

There's a good chance you're not starting your training program from scratch. Look at your existing content to see what you can repurpose: your past training courses, customer knowledge base, case studies, templates, and frameworks.

Your tools can be as high-tech or low-tech as you want, ranging from Word docs to slide decks to interactive training software. However, as we'll discuss more below, multimedia content is more effective than written content alone.

When it comes to experts, you'll likely find those by staring in the mirror. If you're still in startup phase, *you* and your co-founders are probably the experts. If you're not an expert in the training you're conducting, talk with your advisors or hire a consultant. Training your team well is worth every penny.

Principles

"Learners will only remember a handful of things," said Barry, "so take the time to clarify the top three to five takeaways you want them to leave with."

These three to five main takeaways are your principles. You can also think of them as buckets of knowledge you need your team to acquire. For example, when I finally identified the learning principles for WeContent's freelance writers, they were:

1. Client's brand voice

2. Conducting research
3. Creating outlines
4. WeContent's writing style

These principles will eventually turn into chapters or modules in your training program.

Prior knowledge

Last, but not least, you need to figure out what your trainees *know* and *don't know* about your business. In education parlance, this is called "levels of prior knowledge."

Hopefully you've hired a competent team who knows their jobs and industry well. But don't take for granted all the nuances of *your* particular business. This was the trap I fell into when building WeContent's writing team: my writers knew how to write, but they didn't know how to write for *WeContent's* clients in *WeContent's* style.

So before building your training program, make a list of everything your team should already know before getting started. Then make a list of things they don't know. This will become the outline for the next section: key learning outcomes.

When in doubt, err on the side of caution and cover the basics, which aren't always as basic as you expect.

2. KEY LEARNING OUTCOMES

With your building blocks in place, it's time to start creating new material. But don't just dive into the first module. Before you start writing, you need to identify your *key learning outcomes.*

Key learning outcomes, or KLOs, are what you want your audience to be able to do differently after completing each section.

Each section of your training program should focus on a single learning outcome. Learning outcomes can range from remembering factual information (i.e., definitions) to creating new solutions to complex problems. Your KLOs depend on your team's level of prior knowledge. Less-experienced trainees should start with learning factual information, while veterans can jump straight into more challenging tasks.

For a great example of well-defined KLOs, check out The HubSpot Academy, a free online training portal for marketers, salespeople, and customer success professionals. For example, their course on website optimization is split into five lessons. The first video is simply titled, "The Importance of Website Performance." The learning outcome for this video is crystal clear: after watching the video, the viewer should understand the importance of website performance for their company.

Creating KLOs does not need to be complicated. Barry's team uses the tried-and-true SMART framework to develop KLOs for their clients:

- **Specific**—What will your trainee be able to do differently after this lesson?
- **Measurable**—How will you know your KLO has been achieved? For example, HubSpot Academy uses quizzes after each lesson.

- **Attainable**—Can your audience realistically achieve the KLO given their level of prior knowledge?
- **Relevant**—Will the KLO have a positive impact on your audience's work or life?
- **Time-bound**—How long should it take to achieve the KLO?

At the end of each section, your audience should be able to do one thing differently than before. Get clear on what you want that one thing to be.

3. DELIVERY FORMAT

I was never very good or interested in science. But in the seventh grade I learned a lesson I'll never forget:

The Scientific Classifications of Living Things:

- Kingdom
- Phylum
- Class
- Order
- Family
- Genus
- Species

I still remember this completely useless list some twenty-plus years after learning it. Why? Because my science teacher, Mrs. F., had us recite the list in a dozen different silly voices. First we said it like a mouse. Then like a lion. Then we said it like we were sipping tea with the Queen of England. Then we sang it like rockstars. With each silly voice, the list was further lodged into my brain. It will stick with me forever.

You probably had similar experiences in school with unique learning methods. It goes to show that *how* you teach something is just as important as *what* you teach.

Effective training programs combine the right material with the right *delivery format*. Choosing the right format goes back to your building blocks: resources, tools, and experts at your disposal. Will your training be primarily written or video-based? Will lessons be self-paced and online, or live and in-person? Will you prioritize group training or individual learning?

Generally speaking, the more complex the learning material, the more hands-on the training should be. Trainees should have access to experts who can answer nuanced questions and a cohort of peers with whom to collaborate on work. If your trainees are still learning the basics, you can use self-paced, online training. This is HubSpot Academy's approach.

The best training programs use a variety of delivery formats to appeal to every type of learner. This is called a "blended" approach—incorporating visual, audio, written, hands-on, and collaborative learning styles into one lesson. Even the most basic training materials can be improved with multimedia content.

The tone of your training is also important. Think back to my science teacher's unique approach—it wasn't just the delivery format that made it so effective (call and response), but the fun and silly tone.

Do you want your training material to feel formal or informal? Collaborative or instructional? Authoritative or explanatory? Your tone should fit your culture and seriousness of the lesson. Reciting lessons in silly voices probably won't work in a room full of investment bankers (but it might in a marketing agency).

Delivery is everything in teaching. Choose wisely.

4. STORYBOARDING

With your building blocks, learning outcomes, and delivery format in place, it's now time to build the actual lesson. Barry calls this process "storyboarding."

"We believe that the best educators are storytellers because they inspire learning with imagination, teaching us to visualize and think about things instead of simply presenting us with information," said Barry.

Craft your lesson like you're telling a story. Curious Lion recommends a narrative framework that looks like this:

- **Hook**—Capture attention (Again, see Chapter 3).
- **Signpost**—Alert to what's coming and why the person should care.
- **Sensitize**—Be consistent in your choice of music, color, and images to create a receptive mindset.
- **Elucidate**—Explain the more complex topics with definitions and examples.
- **Reinforce**—Repeat key points early and often.
- **Conclude**—Present dramatic climax and summarize key points.

Start writing your lesson by using a bulleted outline. Fill in each of these steps with the written, visual, and interactive material you plan to use. If you're creating visual learning material, Barry recommends using a storyboarding template. Search online for "storyboarding template" for a wide variety of options.

You won't get your storyboarding right on the first try. After creating the first draft, do a dry run of the lesson with a colleague. When you first present the lesson to trainees, note the questions they ask so you can improve your material for next time.

5. REINFORCEMENT

The last step of any good learning program is reinforcement. You've worked hard to teach your audience something new; don't waste that effort by failing to follow up.

"[Reinforcement] is becoming increasingly important in a world in which remote work is the new normal for most companies," said Barry.

As a trainer, give your audience a chance to practice what they've just learned. Use case studies and role playing to reinforce new behaviors. If the lesson is more hands-on, such as fielding customer support phone calls, give trainees real-life reps and review with them afterward.

Your team also needs time to talk with you or the expert. Build in Q&A time, facilitated discussions, coaching and mentoring, and case studies where the expert and learners work through problems together. For additional help and support, encourage your audiences to give feedback to each other. Help them set up a "buddy system" for peer-to-peer learning.

My favorite form of reinforcement is—you guessed

it—writing. Have your trainees write an essay, or even a series of essays, teaching *someone else* the lessons they just learned and how to apply them to their work. Writing forces you to understand the material on a deeper level than conversation alone does. This exercise also creates a paper trail for your trainees to refer back to.

LEARNING FROM MY FAILURE, SO YOU DON'T HAVE TO

In the aftermath of WeContent's blog post debacle, I took a hard look at the way I ran my business. It was clear I had set my team up for failure. Instead of training them on my editorial standards, I threw them into the ocean without a raft. The curse of knowledge bit me hard, and it almost cost me my business.

So when I hired a new freelance writer six months later, I made sure they'd be ready. I wrote a detailed creative brief for each article to serve as their training material. Coincidentally, this document included all the same steps as Curious Lion's training development approach:

- **Building blocks**—My client's mission, brand positioning, value proposition, and product descriptions; word count requirement; and links to relevant prior research and blog posts
- **Learning outcomes**—Blog post objective and target audience description
- **Delivery format**—Tone and style guide
- **Storyboard**—Blog post outline
- **Reinforcement**—Blog post call-to-action

Most importantly, I spent hours giving detailed feedback to the writer, especially on his first few articles. Because sharing information is not enough. True learning comes from trial and error. Which is probably why, even had I known Andrew Barry in 2018, I still might not have heeded his advice on training my team. That was a lesson I had to learn the hard way, but you don't.

Great founders teach and train.

FREE TOOL #3 BONUS:
How to Create a Perfect Digital Training
[ebook]

Training is one of your most vital jobs as a founder. Don't leave it up to chance. Go to **www.curious-lionlearning.com/ebook** to download a free ebook from Andrew Barry, "How to Create a Perfect Digital Training."

PART 2

WRITE WITH EMPATHY

"*Empathy has no script. There is no right way or wrong way to do it. It's simply listening, holding space, withholding judgment, emotionally connecting, and communicating that incredibly healing message of 'You're not alone.'*"

—BRENÉ BROWN

KILL YOUR EGO

How to Destroy a Brand in Four Words

Ratan Tata—the former chairman of India's third largest automaker, Tata Motors—was traveling home from work one day in 2003 when he noticed something that disturbed him.

It was a dark and rainy evening. While Mr. Tata was safe in his luxury vehicle, he saw a family of three dangerously riding through the muddy streets of Mumbai on a two-wheeler. In India, electric bikes and mopeds are three times more popular than automobiles, so this sight was not unusual. But it sparked an idea in Mr. Tata—an opportunity to help India's burgeoning middle class... and mint a new fortune in the process.

What if Tata Motors created a car that was as affordable as a moped?

Mr. Tata became obsessed with the idea and made an impassioned pitch to his board. The company got to work soon after. Over five hundred engineers spent more than four years designing a vehicle that wasn't just comfortable and safe, but extremely affordable. When the Tata Nano was unveiled in 2008, industry analysts hailed it as a miracle of business and engineering. Best of all, it cost just $3,000 USD. Pundits were already declaring victory for Tata.

Yet despite a massive marketing effort, sales of the Tata Nano never reached expectations. Its popularity fizzled quickly after the launch. By 2017, the company halted regular manufacturing and only made the vehicles to order. In 2018, they made just one unit—a *single* Tata Nano rolled off the manufacturing line.

Tata Motors only ever produced 300,000 Nanos. By comparison, *one* Toyota factory in Georgetown, Kentucky, makes over 550,000 Camrys every year. The Nano was an unmitigated failure.

How did things go so wrong?

"THE WORLD'S CHEAPEST CAR"

The logic behind the project was sound. There were millions of Indian families who needed an affordable car, and the Nano had everything they could ever want. But no one bought it. Ironically, the Nano was most popular among rich businessmen. They bought it as a toy—a gimmick to show off to their friends. You can imagine Mr. Tata's frustration. He built exactly what the people of India needed—or so he thought. Was it possible he missed something?

Turns out, the Tata Nano was doomed from the moment it was announced. When Mr. Tata unveiled the

Nano at the Auto Expo in 2008, it was accompanied by a horrendously out-of-touch slogan:

"The World's Cheapest Car."

In rapidly developing India, buying a vehicle was a status symbol for upwardly mobile families. It wasn't just a practical purchase, but a highly emotional one. With those four words, the Nano positioned itself as a car for poor people. Any self-respecting person would rather keep their moped than drive "the world's cheapest car."

Here's a clip from the *Economic Times* about the Nano's early advertising:

> *"It wasn't just for people who would have to stretch to get a car; it could also have been for the housewife or a youngster who'd just turned 18. But the advertising focused at a parity level. It was not aspirational to the one and not desirable to the other two."*

Mr. Tata built the right car at the right moment, but he failed to build something much more important: empathy. Driven by ego, Tata couldn't see the condescending tone of his slogan. He wasn't empowering the people of India; he thought he was saving them. *You're too poor to afford something nice,* he seemed to say, *so here's the world's cheapest car. You're welcome.*

The market responded bitterly to this insult, and Tata Nano sales plummeted.

THINK SMALL

Could the Nano's fate have been different? Luckily, we don't have to imagine too hard. History gives us a near-perfect comparison—another small, affordable car built for the upwardly mobile masses:

The Volkswagen Beetle.

In the 1950s, Volkswagen aspired to break into the American market where big cars reigned supreme. They hired ad executive Bill Bernbach—one of the original "Mad Men" of Madison Avenue—to develop the Beetle's first advertising campaign.

Bernbach was struck by the honesty of the Beetle. It wasn't trying to be anything it wasn't. It was small, well-built, affordable, and didn't take itself too seriously. Bernbach's first ad tried to capture this honesty and paired it with a bit of self-deprecating humor. It took America by storm:

Think small.

Bernbach's approach was genius. He took the Beetle's greatest potential weakness—its size—and made it its greatest strength. The ad lists all the benefits of "thinking small," such as great gas mileage, small repair bills, long-lasting tires, and fitting into tight parking spots. Best of all, the Beetle had no ego. It poked fun at itself. It was quirky and a little rebellious, just like America's freedom-loving youth.

The ad was an instant hit, and so was the Beetle. While American car manufacturers rolled out yacht-sized sedans, Volkswagen's tiny Beetle won the heart of America's fast-growing counterculture. The campaign ran for over a decade, with each ad highlighting a unique "benefit" of the Beetle:

"Lemon."

"It's ugly, but it gets you there."

"And if you run out of gas, it's easy to push."

"Not to be confused with a cheetah."

One thing you never saw in the Beetle ads?

"Cheap."

Yes, the Beetle was affordable, but Bernbach knew it stood for so much more.

Tata Motors should have learned a lot from the Beetle's success. Before the launch of the Nano, focus groups said they liked the car's ability to park in tight spaces. Tata could have borrowed a few lines of copy directly from the "Think Small" ad—likely to great success.

In fact, the Beetle's famous ad campaign was a perfect template for marketing the Nano. Bernbach brilliantly highlighted the *feeling* of owning a Volkswagen Beetle: The *joy* of finding a small parking space only you can fit in. The *relief* of seeing that small insurance bill that leaves money in your pocket.

Tata, on the other hand, made a purely rational pitch for the Nano: it's cheap. No matter how tight your budget, *no one* wants to be seen as cheap. (Unless you're already rich; in that case, you may wear cheap as a badge of honor, just like the businessmen who bought the Nano.)

Bernbach understood something that Mr. Tata failed to grasp: buying a car is a huge life moment for most people—even if the car is small and affordable. Volkswagen turned this moment into a movement. After the "Think Small" ad was released, teenagers ripped it out of magazines and pinned it up on their wall. The Nano became the butt of jokes.

COULD EMPATHY HAVE SAVED THE TATA NANO?

In 2015, after a massive decline in demand, the Nano team rebranded.

They scrapped their price-aggressive language and positioned the Nano as a fast, fun, easy car for free-loving young people (sound familiar?) Commercials featured young adults, laughing and carrying guitars, driving out of their way for their favorite street food. They drove to the beach, to parties, and cruised with friends down beautiful coastal streets. The ads focused on the experience of owning a Nano. But did it work?

Marketing consultant Nauby Gupta thought the new campaign was too little, too late. "[The Nano] has been positioned as a price-aggressive product," he said in an article from *The Economic Times*, "You can't get away from that."

The new campaign was a success from a creative standpoint, but it didn't help the Nano's sales. In 2018, Tata discontinued the Nano for good.

The Nano's last gasp teaches us one final lesson: you rarely get a second chance to make the right first impression. Negative emotions are like a tattoo on the heart—they stay with your audience, even if you later change your tone.

The Nano could have been India's most iconic vehicle. Instead, The World's Cheapest Car is no more.

Great founders, like great writers, put aside their ego and work hard to build empathy with their audience. And that's exactly what empathy is: emotional work. Being rational is easy. Understanding what your audience really wants—what they *need*—is hard.

As a founder, empathy starts with you. Let's look at how to build deeper relationships with your customers and audience.

$$6$$

KNOW THY READER

How to Build Empathy in Six Questions

When Brian Chesky and Joe Gebbia, the founders of Airbnb, arrived at the Y Combinator headquarters in San Francisco, they received a shocking piece of advice that would change their lives.

The co-founder of YC, Paul Graham, asked the founders a seemingly innocent question: "Where do your customers live?" There weren't many at the time, but they said Airbnb had a cluster of early adopters in New York City.

"Then what the hell are you doing here?" Graham asked. "Get on a plane and go talk to your customers."

How could they refuse? For months, Chesky and Gebbia made the grueling weekly commute between San Francisco and New York. They talked with every early customer on the platform while living in Airbnbs themselves. This experience gave them invaluable insights, such as the importance of good photography for every listing. Airbnb began to flourish in New York, and later, across the country.

Could Chesky and Gebbia have learned the same lessons by calling or surveying their customers? No chance. By visiting the homes of their early hosts, the Airbnb founders did so much more than just "talk" to their customers. They saw their lives on and off the platform. They walked a mile in their shoes—or in this case, literally slept a night on their couch. Airbnb didn't invent the concept of couch surfing, but they made it mainstream by nailing the tiny details, such as providing up to one million dollars of damage protection for each listing. Hosts didn't ask for this, but through hours of conversation, Chesky and Gebbia realized they *needed* it for their peace of mind.

That's the power of empathy.

"Get to know your customers" is such common startup advice that we can easily forget what it really means. It's not about compiling demographics and creating fictional buyer personas. It's about having intimate conversations to understand what your customers really want, need, and what stands in their way from getting it. To serve your customers, you need to know what they truly care about and what they don't and prioritize ruthlessly.

The same is true when writing. Knowing your reader's occupation and LinkedIn credentials isn't enough. To build massive empathy, you need to sleep a night on their couch (or whatever your equivalent is).

Ultimately, there are six questions you need to answer to really *Know Thy Reader*:

1. Who am I writing to?
2. What do they want?
3. What do they *need*?
4. What stands in their way?
5. How can I help?
6. Why should they care?

These questions, of course, also apply to knowing thy customer. Because for founders, your readers and customers are often one in the same.

Let's dig into each question.

1. Who am I writing to?

Julianne Putano, my sister, recently broke free from the corporate world and started her own wellness studio. She teaches yoga, Thai massage, and Reiki energy therapy. As a new founder, Julianne is experiencing firsthand the challenge of not just delivering services, but attracting the right customers, leasing studio space, and managing finances.

But Julianne's goal is not to build a wellness empire. Instead, she wants the freedom to do work she loves and to help people. She's actively downsizing her lifestyle to fit this dream. She pictures a day when she lives in a tiny house and tends to her garden while teaching classes full of enthusiastic students on her own schedule. This is not the typical entrepreneurial dream, but it's hers.

Why am I telling you this? Because Julianne is one of the people I wrote this book for. I had her name listed at the top of my first draft like I was writing a letter to her.

David Perell, a writing coach and author, says, "Write

for one obsessive person... Writing comes alive at the extremes."

In other words, if you try to write to everyone, you'll speak to no one.

The best writing happens when you write to a specific person or two. Not the perfect version of them, but the *real* them—their fears, flaws, dreams, and all. That person stands in proxy of every other potential reader. By focusing on your one reader, your writing will feel personal. Your readers will get the sense you actually know them, and they'll start to think they know you, too.

Tim Ferriss used this strategy while writing *The 4-Hour Workweek*. After struggling to find his voice in the first draft, Ferriss decided to write to two close friends who wanted to escape the nine-to-five grind. To enhance the illusion, Ferriss literally wrote his next chapter in an email addressed to his friends. The trick worked. *The 4-Hour Workweek* became a number one *New York Times* bestseller.

The more specific you are about who you're writing to, the stronger your writing will be. That's why I recommend writing to someone you actually know. It could be a friend, colleague, or a customer willing to spend time with you.

Let's look at an example:

Imagine, like Julianne, you're building a wellness studio. You decide to add career coaching to your list of services. Your first task is to create a landing page to test your messaging and find a few early customers to try out the service.

Now ask yourself: *Who am I writing to?*

You want to work with creative entrepreneurs. But

this is a large and diverse group. If you try to write to everyone, you'll end up with a shapeless gray blob of a landing page. Your service will resonate with no one. If you focus on one obsessive person, your landing page will explode with life, clarity, and passion.

You choose to write to your friend Sandy, a veteran sales rep who wants to start a pottery business. She's already started an online Etsy store but dreams of opening a small studio in the heart of Ohio City, Cleveland. She's nervous to leave the comforts of her full-time job and worries about money. She needs a plan—and a little courage—to make the leap.

Forget writing for all creative entrepreneurs. You're writing for Sandy.

When you decide who you're writing to, put their name at the top of your draft. Or, like Ferriss, draft an email to them. Do whatever you need to convince yourself you're writing to one person.

Once you're crystal-clear on your reader, let's get to know them a little better.

2. *What do they want?*

We all have goals and desires.

Some of us want financial independence. Others want to travel. Some people dream of a simpler life, while others want adventure. Many people want to go back to the way things used to be—back to when they were happier, healthier, and had fewer worries in the world.

When your reader tells you what they want, listen to them. But keep in mind, this is *not* the most important thing you'll learn about them, and it shouldn't be the *only* thing, either. But knowing what your reader wants is a great starting point. You can use this information to pique their interest.

Think about Sandy, your friend who wants to open a pottery studio. What are her goals? Does she want to build a pottery empire or a small lifestyle business? What does success mean to her?

Humans are never satisfied for long. Virtually everyone wants more of something. It's your job to identify the thing they want and help them get it.

But there's a big difference between what your reader *wants* and what they *need*.

3. *What do they need?*

Most people are very good at telling you what they want: money, free time, adventure, independence.

But most of us are less adept at knowing what we *need*. Our needs, both physical and psychological, sit just below the surface of our consciousness. We don't know we need something until we get it, or it's suddenly taken away.

Let's talk about your friend, Sandy. She wants to leave her corporate job and open a pottery studio. But what does she *need* to make this happen?

Amazingly, there are only eight things humans really *need*. Copywriter and author Drew Eric Whitman compiled a list of these needs in his book, *Cashvertising* (cringey name, great book on copywriting.)

He calls them The Lifeforce 8:

1. Survival

2. Sustenance (i.e., food and water)
3. Freedom from pain and fear
4. Sexual companionship
5. Comfortable living (i.e., peace of mind)
6. Achievement and winning
7. Caring for loved ones
8. Social acceptance

Then there are secondary motivations, which are less powerful but very common in our developed world. Whitman calls them "learned" motivations. There are nine in total:

1. To be informed
2. Curiosity
3. Cleanliness of body and surroundings
4. Efficiency
5. Convenience
6. Dependability/quality
7. Expression of beauty and style
8. Economy/profit
9. Bargains

These lists help explain why Tata Nano failed so spectacularly. Mr. Tata appealed to the weakest possible motivator—bargains—while ignoring primary needs like achievement and social acceptance. The Volkswagen Beetle, on the other hand, appealed to comfortable living, social acceptance, convenience, dependability, and self-expression. Affordability was hardly mentioned—it wasn't necessary.

Now, back to Sandy. What does she *need*? Start at the

top of the Lifeforce 8 list and work your way down. Right away you'll see fundamental needs to address: survival and sustenance. For humans, a lack of money signals danger. Sandy needs to know she will not go hungry or lose her home if she starts her own business.

But that's not all. She's used to a certain level of comfort from her nine-to-five job. That's at risk of going away when she quits. She's not even sure she'll succeed. It would be easier to not try at all. And what will her friends and family think if she starts a pottery studio? Will they accept her decision or call her crazy and irresponsible?

As you already know, becoming an entrepreneur is a loaded decision. It's wrapped up in multiple fundamental needs that Sandy must satisfy before taking the leap. Your landing page should address each one of these needs specifically and explain how you help clients overcome them.

Your reader won't tell you what they need, so it will take some digging to uncover. But once you do, you're well on your way to building massive empathy.

Next, you need to identify and address what's standing in their way.

4. What stands in their way?

You now have a clear idea of who your reader is, what they want, and what they need. Now let's find out what's standing in their way: the obstacles, blind spots, villains, and forces of nature that may stop them from reaching their goals.

By recognizing the obstacles standing in your reader's way, you're saying to them, "You don't have to fight this alone. We're on the same team. It's us versus the world, and we're going to win."

That's the definition of empathy: to understand and share the feelings of another—especially in the face of uncertainty.

Most obstacles fall into one of two categories: villains and mountains. Villains are forces trying to hurt your reader. They can be internal or external, but the pain is usually immediate and acute. Mountains are challenges for your reader to overcome. They are opportunities for your reader to grow and become the best version of themselves—to achieve something great.

What stands in Sandy's way from opening her pottery studio? Her villains are self-doubt and a well-meaning family member trying to hold her back. She's also worried about competing with a more established pottery studio in town. Sandy's mountains include growing her savings from six months to eighteen months, finding a studio space, and learning how to market her new business.

The best way to address your reader's obstacles is to turn them into advantages, just like Bill Burnbach did with the Volkswagen Beetle. You can help Sandy harness her self-doubt and use it as motivation to learn more quickly. Show her how to turn that "competing" pottery studio into a collaborator.

Make a list of all the potential villains and mountains standing in your reader's way. Next, you'll help them turn those obstacles into opportunities.

5. *How can I help?*

The first four questions you just answered were research. Now it's time to turn those insights into action.

Your reader is facing down villains and mountains on the way to achieving their wildest dreams. What can you do to help? Remember the lesson from Tata Motors: you are not a savior. Instead, think of yourself as a guide. You provide *maps* to scale mountains and *swords* to slay villains.

The Airbnb founders had dozens of mountains and villains to address (twice as many as a typical business, since they were building a two-sided marketplace). They had to help guests overcome the *mountain* of uncertainty when choosing an Airbnb. They provided professional photography as a *map* for each listing. Airbnb's hosts had to face *villainous* guests stealing or destroying their homes. Chesky and Gebbia gave them a *weapon* to defend themselves in the form of damage protection.

Sandy's villains include her own self-doubt and her mother, who guilts her into staying at her current job. As a career coach, how can you arm Sandy to take on these villains? Your weapons probably include positive self-talk exercises, scripts for having difficult conversations, and a journal for tracking her progress. Sandy's mountains require a different form of assistance. You can help her create a map—a timeline or plan—to build new skills and reach her goal.

Go back to your list of mountains and villains from the previous step. Brainstorm different maps and swords you can provide to help your reader succeed.

6. Why should they care?

Whether you're writing a landing page or an investor memo, your reader will always ask themselves the same question: "Why should I care about this? Why should I spend my precious time on *you*?"

This question should look familiar—we asked the same one in Chapter 3: Sell With Storytelling. I've added it again because it's so important. You've done the hard work of building massive empathy for your reader. Now it's time to distill your insights into a single sentence.

For this question, let's use a tried-and-true exercise to get to the heart of the matter: *The 5 Whys.*

Imagine you're talking to Sandy. You write her an email about your new career coaching service for creative entrepreneurs.

Sandy responds: *"Why should I care about that?"* (1×)

Using your audience research—what you know about Sandy's wants, needs, obstacles, and potential solutions—try to craft a single sentence answer to her question.

> You: *"My coaching service will help you make the leap from corporate life to full-time entrepreneur."*

> Sandy: *"Why should I care about that?"* (2×)

Keep digging to find a deeper answer to the question. The goal is to go 5 Whys deep.

> You: *"To live the passionate, creative life you've always wanted."*

> Sandy: *"Why should I care about that?"* (3×)

You: *"So you can live a life of no regrets."*

Sandy: *"Why should I care about that?"* (4×)

You: *"Because life is short. Live it to the absolute fullest."*

Sandy: *"Why should I care about that?"* (5×)

You: *"So that you live a life that inspires others to live their best lives."*

There it is. Is it the perfect answer to Sandy's question? You won't know for sure until you get feedback from actual customers. But it's a whole lot better than just "Become a full-time entrepreneur."

Building empathy for your reader is hard work. That's why it's so worthwhile—few other founders are doing it. You can stand out from the crowd just by knowing your customers better than your competitors.

As Paul Graham said, "What the hell are you doing here? Go talk to your customers."

And crash on their couch, if they'll let you. It will be time well spent.

FREE TOOL #4 BONUS:
Empathy Builder Template

Empathy for your customers and readers is crucial. Go to **www.greatfounderswrite.com/bonus**, enter your email, then click on "Empathy Builder" to get the free template. Use this framework to write copy for your landing pages, sales emails, paid ads, or content marketing.

$$7$$

FIND THE WIN-WIN OPPORTUNITY

How to Persuade Without Losing Your Soul

M y junior year of college was an odd one.

Living in my fraternity house, I'd regularly stay up until 3:00 or 4:00 a.m. with my friends. Then I'd be up at 6:00 a.m. to head to work at Northwestern Mutual, an insurance and wealth management company. I was an intern, but not the type that made coffee runs and collected mail. I was a licensed insurance agent.

At 7:00 a.m., I'd be in the office for our agent meeting and to hit the phones. The first hour of every day was spent cold-calling strangers to talk about death and money. Like I said, it was an odd year.

But this experience taught me the art of persuasion. I was a college student (and not a very good one) trying to sell life insurance to doctors, lawyers, and families with small kids. Why would they even take a meeting, let alone buy something from me?

It wasn't easy, but I ended up in the top 10 percent of agent interns in the country that year. It was my first taste of making real money (which was quickly wasted), but the lessons learned were far more valuable. As a founder, I use the skills I acquired from that internship every single day.

GREAT FOUNDERS PERSUADE WITH EMPATHY

A founder's job can be distilled to two tasks:

1. To build
2. To persuade

Founders build products, audiences, processes, and teams. For many founders (especially those without a sales background) this is where they stop. "Build it, and they will come" is still a pervasive mindset, even if the founder knows it's not true. Deep down, they hope it's true, because building is what they're good at. Building is in their comfort zone.

What's not in their comfort zone? Persuasion.

Let's take a quiz. On a Scale of 1–10, how comfortable are you with persuading others? Be honest. A 10 means you aren't just comfortable—you find joy in it—whereas a 1 means you avoid persuasion at all costs.

Most founders fall somewhere in the middle. Persuasion is a necessary evil. They do it when they need to, but they avoid it when they can.

Why are so many people uncomfortable with persuasion? Because they confuse persuasion with manipulation. The two things couldn't be more different. Persuasion is the art of finding common ground with someone—a win-win solution. Manipulation is a tactic used to trick a person into a one-sided deal.

Persuasion is rooted in empathy. You need to put yourself in the other person's shoes. The most persuasive people are also the most empathetic. Manipulation is rooted in narcissism. Manipulators don't care about the other person. They are just out for themselves.

The most persuasive people believe deeply in their cause. Their conviction is palpable. They want nothing more than to see their vision become a reality. Manipulators don't really believe in what they're selling. They're in it for the money and power.

The first step to becoming more persuasive is believing there is such a thing as ethical persuasion. If you think persuasion is inherently wrong, you'll never get comfortable with it. To ensure you're persuading ethically and not slipping into manipulation, consider what makes persuasion ethical.

Ethical persuasion has the four following characteristics:

1. **Conviction.** Do I believe deeply in my business and services?
2. **Honesty.** If an objective third party looked at my position, would they conclude that I'm being honest and transparent?

3. **Win-Win.** Is this in the best interest of the other party? If not, how do I create a win-win situation?
4. **Choice.** Does the other person still have a choice? Be sure you aren't backing them into a corner or putting an uncomfortable amount of pressure on them. Ethical persuaders are ok with the final decision no matter what.

Have I persuaded you that ethical persuasion is possible? Good, now let's talk about how to do it.

4 STEPS TO ETHICAL PERSUASION

According to research by Professor Jay Conger (which first appeared in the *Harvard Business Review*), there are four steps to becoming more persuasive in the workplace:

1. Establish credibility
2. Find common ground
3. Use vivid examples
4. Connect emotionally

While this research was conducted on corporate organizations, it applies to startups as well. Let's look at each through the lens of a founder:

1. Establish credibility

Founders inherit a certain level of credibility in their own companies. This is called positional credibility—authority earned by the nature of their role.

But positional credibility can backfire if abused.

Founders who demand or manipulate, rather than per-suade, are not long for the startup world. Your smartest employees will leave, and you'll be stuck with yes-people who don't know what they're doing. Don't rely on posi-tional credibility.

Real credibility is established by deep experience, sound decision-making, listening to feedback, and con-sistently showing up and doing the work.

Credibility is not universal, either. As a technical founder, you have credibility on development decisions, but maybe not marketing or sales decisions. You may have deep experience in one industry (e.g., hospitality), but what happens when your startup pivots to micro-office space? Credibility must be earned in every vertical and every function of the company.

So what do you do when you find yourself wading into an area where you lack credibility? You borrow it. Before presenting your case to the team or investors, build a coalition of people who have deep credibility in that spe-cific area. Ask them questions about the feasibility of your idea, what roadblocks may occur, and why the com-pany should (or should not) take this direction. If the experts are on board, ask them to vouch for your deci-sion. Borrow their credibility to supplement yours.

How do you establish credibility when writing? Same as you would in a presentation or board meeting. Answer the question, "Why should we listen to *you* on this sub-ject?" If you have earned credibility, say why. "I've spent fifteen years in the commercial real estate market." If you haven't earned credibility, cite sources who have it. "Jeanne Gang is a world-renowned architect. Together we developed this plan."

Once you've earned or borrowed the credibility you need, turn your attention to those on the other side of the table.

2. Find common ground

The crux of ethical persuasion is finding common ground—a win-win scenario. Your goal isn't to create the absolute best deal for yourself, but to find a solution that both parties can be satisfied with. You want others to walk away feeling like they could work with you again. Play the long game.

Finding common ground is an act of empathy. Let's revisit the empathy-building questions we asked in Chapter 6:

1. Who am I writing to?
2. What do they want?
3. What do they *need*?
4. What stands in their way?
5. How can I help?
6. Why should they care?

For persuasion, one more question to ask is: "What objections will the other party have?"

Let's say you think you need to shut down a poor-performing product: the Ultra Widget. It's not worth the time and resources your team is putting into it. You need to put more energy toward your best-performing tool (we'll call it the Super Widget). But the Ultra Widget team still believes in its potential and doesn't want to give it up. How do you persuade them it's best to shut it down?

As a founder, you have two options.

Option one: Mandate they shut it down and move on. This path may be quick, but you also risk pissing off a lot of people.

Option two: Make your case. Let's use the questions above to craft a persuasive message:

1. Who am I writing to?

   The Ultra Widget team: Raj, Cecily, and Stephen. They've been working on Ultra Widget for nine months.

2. What do they want?

   The Ultra Widget team wants to continue working on Ultra Widget. It was Stephen's idea in the first place. He recruited Raj and Cecily early on to build it. They believe it can become a game-changing tool for the industry. They want just six more months to prove its value.

3. What do they need?

   The team needs to feel successful. By shutting down Ultra Widget, they may feel like they wasted nine months of work on nothing.

4. What stands in their way?

   Mountain: Ultra Widget has about one-third of the daily active users as the company's most popular tool, Super Widget. Worse yet, user growth has slowed to a crawl.

Villain: They've developed a "failure is not an option" mindset. Raj, Cecily, and Stephen are convinced that if Ultra Widget fails, they will be seen as failures by the company and that they may even lose their jobs. They believe their reputations are at stake.

5. How can I help?

First, the team needs to know a product failure is not personal failure. Are scientists upset when an experiment fails? Of course not! They're elated because they learned something new. The team needs to know their jobs are safe and their time working on Ultra Widget was NOT wasted.

Plus, it hasn't been all bad with Ultra Widget. The team has learned valuable consumer insights and they've developed a few innovative features. We can try to incorporate Ultra Widget's most popular features into Super Widget.

6. Why should they care?

The Ultra Widget team did not fail. They exemplified the startup's mission and are a testament to the incredible things they are building together. Even though Ultra Widget did not succeed, we can use it to propel Super Widget's user growth. If we're all rowing in the same direction, we'll reach our ultimate goal—an IPO—faster.

7. What objections will they have?

    ◦ "What will six more months hurt?"

      It's just not Ultra Widget's slow growth that's a concern. We also need to consider Super Widget's massive growth. We see this as *the* opportunity for us, and we need all hands on deck to succeed. We can't waste any more time pulling in different directions.

    ◦ "What will we tell Ultra Widget's best users?"

      We're incorporating UW's best features into Super Widget. It will be better than ever. But at the end of the day, we can't make everyone happy.

    ◦ "What will we do now?"

      We need you on the Super Widget team.

Notice how we found common ground with the Ultra Widget team. We framed the decision to shut down Ultra Widget as a win-win. The company can now grow faster, and the Ultra Widget team will contribute to this.

Finding this amicable solution wouldn't have been possible without deep empathy. As a founder, you need to understand the emotional impact of your decisions. The best persuaders take emotions into account—they don't try to bulldoze over them in the name of logic and efficiency.

3. Use vivid examples

Sara Blakely had a problem. Before her brand of shapewear, Spanx, became a household name—and before she became the first self-made female billionaire in the U.S.—Blakely couldn't even get her product into stores.

Early customers absolutely loved their Spanx. It solved a problem that long plagued women's clothing, one that many women had found homemade solutions for. But when trying to explain the problem to department store buyers, it never clicked.

On the hit podcast, *How I Built This* with Guy Raz, Blakely shared the story of how she finally got Spanx into Macy's. While meeting with the department store's senior buyer, Blakely couldn't get her to understand the value proposition. Despite the sales figures and customer testimonials, the senior buyer was not convinced.

Finally, out of desperation, Blakely decided to literally show her what Spanx could do. She took the buyer to the nearest restroom and stepped into the stall. She stepped out no longer wearing Spanx under her dress. The senior buyer could instantly see the difference in the way Blakely's dress fit her. Macy's started selling Spanx immediately.

Blakely, like all great persuaders, understood that vivid examples are more convincing than numbers.

As a writer, you can use stories to add vivid examples to your work. I opened this book with a story about Benjamin Franklin. If you remember anything from reading *Great Founders Write,* I would bet it's that story (but I hope it's much more). Stories stick in our brains better than facts and figures, which makes them potent tools for persuasion.

Don't get me wrong: numbers are still critical to crafting a persuasive argument. But they aren't enough on their own. Use numbers to *justify* your argument, not make it.

4. Connect emotionally

Suneel Gupta—entrepreneur and author of *Backable*—spent years researching what it takes to raise venture capital. Gupta saw that some founders had that "It" factor... but what was it?

After years of researching the question, Gupta discovered that the most persuasive founders had one thing in common: *conviction*. They believed deeply in their cause and company.

Contrary to popular belief, people aren't persuaded by logic—they're convinced by emotion. People want to see you are emotionally committed to your venture. You don't just believe it in your head—you believe it in your heart and soul.

But emotion is a two-way street. You also need to understand the emotional state of your audience. What type of energy should you use to present your new idea? Should you go in strong and opinionated, or soft and guiding? If you get the emotional tone wrong, you'll lose your audience immediately.

Go back to Chapter 6, question #3: What does your audience *need*? Do they need reassurance that they're livelihood is safe? Are they craving novelty or self-expression? Use this question to probe the emotional state of your audience and connect with them on their level.

PRACTICING PERSUASION

Persuasion is an art. Like all art, it's rooted in empathy. Your goal is not to win, but to create a win-win scenario for you and others involved.

There's one last thing to keep in mind about persuasion: it takes practice. As a life insurance agent, I would literally role-play sales conversations with my boss to hone my persuasion skills. We'd also review after meetings and phone calls to identify what I did well and where I could improve.

I recommend keeping a journal of your persuasive conversations. Record the details of the situation, what went well, and where you could improve. What objections came up? What did you learn about the other party that could help you create a better win-win solution? What facts or vivid examples could you add to strengthen your position?

When you really believe in something, persuasion will no longer feel like a necessary evil. It will feel like a natural step in the journey of building your vision.

NURTURE KEY RELATIONSHIPS

How to Write to Your Investors, Stakeholders, and Biggest Champions

Mac Conwell is a developer, two-time startup founder, and venture capitalist. In 2020 he started Rarebreed Ventures, a pre-seed fund focused on under-represented founders—female founders, minority founders, and founders living outside the main startup hubs in the U.S.

For all of Mac's skills as a developer and capital allo-cator, his greatest strength (in my opinion) is his sto-rytelling. As we discussed the importance of founder-investor communications, he shared this story:

"When I worked for the state of Maryland venture fund, we had a high-flying startup who had just landed a major distribution deal. Things were going great, but then we didn't hear from them for a while. I went about my business, working other deals and such. Then one day I got an email from one of the co-founders."

Mac seemed visibly shaken at this moment, as if he was reliving the experience while telling me the story. For an investor, surprise emails are about as welcome as kidney stones.

The email said, "Hey Mac, just thought you should know. Our CEO took another job at a marketing agency. Also, we're out of money."

"*Just thought I should know?*" Mac asked rhetorically. "Um, yeah, I think I should know!"

Mac called the co-founder within minutes of receiving the email. Apparently the company blew their budget on R&D and didn't have enough money for production. Mac helped them acquire new capital to temporarily salvage the situation, but they continued to fall into debt and eventually went under.

"Because they spent so much time trying to solve the problem themselves, by the time they told me about it, I could no longer help them," said Mac.

As a founder, people are betting on you to be smart and resourceful. So when a problem arises, it's tempting to keep it quiet and try to solve it on your own. Sometimes you will, but it could also cost you your company.

Mac then shared another story with me, this time about one of his portfolio founders whose communication skills saved the company, and potentially much more.

The founder was an immigrant living in the U.S. One day he was met at his home by ICE agents and was taken into custody. There was a misunderstanding about his immigration status. The founder called Mac immediately:

"Hey Mac, I'm being taken away right now. Just wanted you to hear it from me and not my co-founder."

Then he hung up.

It was a Friday. Mac had planned on a quiet weekend of work and rest, but plans had changed. He dropped everything and started making calls. Mac found a better lawyer for the founder, and they were able to clear up the confusion. The founder was released and the matter resolved by the end of the weekend.

"Had he waited to call me until Monday, the situation would've been completely different," said Mac.

If you find the right investors, they will do whatever they can to help you succeed. But they aren't mind readers. Frequent, honest communication is the foundation of a beneficial founder-investor relationship.

4 HABITS OF GREAT RELATIONSHIP BUILDERS

According to Mac, great founders share four communication habits that help them build strong relationships with their investors:

1. When in doubt, over-communicate

In the first story Mac shared with me, the founder suffered from a common problem: under-communication.

"Come to me with solutions, not problems," is still the pervasive mindset in business, despite it being thoroughly debunked by organizational researchers. When times get tough, many founders and business leaders go quiet until they find a solution to share. They don't want to look incompetent or panicky by raising the alarm.

But many founders under-communicate during good times as well. They don't want to brag or talk about "little" wins. This is also a mistake.

"The founders that I have the best relationships with tend to be those that over-communicate. They text me. They tell me the good AND the bad, right when it happens," said Mac.

When in doubt, the best founders over-communicate. The habit of sharing everything—good and bad—has several benefits. First, over-communication gives investors more opportunities to help you. They can only assist if they know what's going on with you and your business. Second, over-communication saves investors from being surprised by bad news. Surprises destroy trust, and a lack of trust is the root of all relationship problems. Finally, over-communication keeps you accountable. Sharing your intentions will improve your chances of following through. Tell your investors what you're going to do, then do it.

Is there a limit to over-communication? It's different for every investor, but their patience is a lot higher than you might think. "As an investor, it's my job to tell you, 'Hey, you don't need to text me every day. Let's keep it to once a week unless something big happens.'" said Mac. "But even then, you could come back at me and say, 'Don't you want us to succeed?' and I'll probably let it slide."

When in doubt, over-communicate.

2. Be consistent

On the surface, writing consistent investor memos doesn't seem all that important, especially if you're already over-communicating with your investors informally.

But keeping a consistent routine is valuable for two reasons.

First, consistency is a trust-building exercise. There's that word again: *trust*. If you're organized and responsible enough to send out an email at the same time each month, you're likely organized in all aspects of your work.

The second reason is that consistency breeds self-confidence. Much of our success is determined by our personal view of ourselves. Do you believe you're a good leader? A strong communicator? A reliable person? The way we view ourselves is critical, and we can start to view ourselves more positively by succeeding in small ways on a consistent basis.

By being consistent with something like investor memos, you start to see yourself as a person who is consistent and reliable. This will bleed into other areas of your life and work.

This is a lesson I had to learn the hard way. After years of holding myself back with negative self-talk, I decided to try to change my habits instead of my thoughts. I committed to a daily exercise routine, which gave me confidence in every aspect of my life. It also, slowly but surely, shifted my self-talk from negative to positive.

Be consistent. Choose a manageable cadence for your investor updates and show up.

3. Share the good, but especially the bad

Investors don't want to be the last to know about good news. They're not just financially invested in your success, but emotionally as well. Sharing your wins is a great moment for you and your biggest supporters.

But sharing bad news is far more important. When a crisis hits, start talking.

Many founders wait to tell investors about a problem until after it's solved. This is always a mistake. There's no guarantee you can solve the crisis on your own. We saw the tragic consequences of under-communication earlier in the chapter.

But also, you miss out on a chance to tell your adventurous story. Great startups are defined by the crises they overcome. These stories become legendary and part of the myth surrounding your company. Your investors will share your story far and wide, but only if they are part of the action.

Bottom line: keep investors in the loop as problems come and go.

4. Use stories to bring the numbers to life

We've talked about the power of stories throughout this book, and they are just as powerful in your investor updates.

"Whenever I write an update to my Limited Partners [the folks who invest in Rarebreed Ventures], I start with a story," said Mac. "It's usually about a founder we recently invested in. I share their mission, why they built the company, what makes them amazing, and why we invested. It gives my investors a much better feel for the work we're doing. It brings the numbers to life."

Starting investor updates with a story is a little unusual, Mac admits. Most begin with top-line and bottom-line numbers. But sharing personal stories in your investor updates can help your investors build an emotional connection not just to you, but your customers and mission.

Inspire with stories. Convince with numbers.

GREAT RELATIONSHIPS START WITH YOU

Good communication builds trust, and trust builds relationships. This is true with your team as much as your investors. If you've chosen the right investors—those who bring more to the table than just money—then you want as close a relationship as possible to them.

"The more you communicate with your investors, the more value you'll get out of them," said Mac.

Yes, VCs have a financial incentive to see you succeed. But it's *you* who needs to lead the relationship. Share your wins, losses, and challenges on a regular basis. Model the type of communication you want and that's what you'll receive in return.

PART 3:
WRITE WITH CLARITY

"Clutter is the disease of American writing. We are a society strangling in unnecessary words, circular constructions, pompous frills, and meaningless jargon."

—WILLIAM ZINSSER

$$9$$

MAKE EVERY WORD COUNT

How to Turn Clarity Into a Competitive Advantage

Natalie is the CEO of an enterprise SaaS startup (real names have been changed to protect the guilty).

Every Monday morning, after making her coffee, Natalie checks her company's Stripe dashboard to review their Net Monthly Recurring Revenue (Net MRR), the company's North Star metric. It's lower than she expected to see, so she shoots a direct message to her Head of Growth, Miguel.

> *"Hey Miguel, what's the status on our Q3 Net MRR? We're already a month in and don't seem to be on track to reach the target. We need to keep up the pace or we're going to get lapped. Let me know what I can do to help."*

Miguel is just getting ready for his week when he gets a push notification on his phone. It's from Natalie. Miguel reads the message. Then he reads it again. *What does she mean by "we're going to get lapped?"* He feels his adrenaline rising and his heart starts to race. As the head of growth, the buck stops with him. It's his ass on the line if they don't hit their Net MRR.

So Miguel copies Natalie's message to his growth team's Slack channel and DM's the product team lead as well. He adds the note:

> *"This month is critical for us. Net MRR is our top priority. We have to keep pushing. Let me know what you need from me."*

The company's sales, marketing, and engineering teams all read the message. Their collective panic rises.

What does Miguel mean by, "Net MRR is our top priority?" they wonder. *Do we need to change our focus, or just keep doing what we're doing?*

What does it mean for Chris, the senior product manager, whose team has been working for six weeks on a highly requested customer feature? What about Adam, the director of marketing, who is halfway through a co-branding campaign with a channel partner? What does it mean for Nikki, the new director of sales, who has been nurturing enterprise opportunities but is still a month or two away from filling her pipeline?

Natalie's message seemed harmless at first glance. She asked one of her team leads about a major quarterly goal. But in reality, she's caused a wave of uncertainty throughout her company. Her lack of clarity raised more questions than her team could possibly answer.

BATTLING CHAOS WITH CLARITY

Being a startup founder is a stressful and lonely job. When the pressure is on, we tend to "act now and think later," a survival instinct that keeps us safe from snakes... only to run straight into a den of lions.

In times of high pressure and uncertainty, one leadership trait is more valuable than any other: clarity.

Clear communication is the knife that cuts through chaos, giving you and your team a direction and a plan. It focuses your limited resources like a laser aimed at the single most important thing. Clarity brings sanity back to insane situations.

Meanwhile, a *lack* of clarity amplifies the chaos with every layer of management it passes through. Like a game of telephone, the message becomes so obscured it ceases to resemble the original intention.

In some high-stress situations, miscommunication means death. SWAT teams, emergency room staff, and air traffic control groups are some of the most effective teams on the planet. One reason is that they obsess over precise language. Every word and phrase means exactly one thing, and they always confirm with each other that they understand.

Miscommunication in business is not typically a life-or-death situation, but it can certainly kill your company.

Let's go over Natalie's message again. She used several words and phrases that lacked clear, singular meanings:

- **"Status"**—Natalie had the Stripe dashboard right in front of her, so what type of update was she looking for?
- **"Keep up the pace"**—Keep up the pace of what?
- **"We're going to get lapped"**—Is Natalie talking about competitors, or is this a veiled threat to Miguel's job?
- **"Let me know what I can do to help"**—What is Natalie really willing to do to help? This sounds more like an empty gesture than a genuine offer of support.

Miguel, when relaying the message to the growth and product teams, increased the confusion by using phrases like "Top priority" and "Keep pushing."

Founders and startup leaders don't intentionally send their teams into chaos with unclear communication. We assume (often wrongly) that everyone understands what we mean by certain phrases. *You* know what you mean when you say "top priority" but your product manager has a different definition.

Clear communication has never been more important, especially as more teams shift to distributed and remote work. You can no longer rely on body language, back channels, and the familiarity that comes from working in an office together.

What does clear writing look like, and how can you achieve clarity on a regular basis? A little planning before firing off that message goes a long way.

CLEAR WRITING STARTS WITH A CLEAR PURPOSE

There are many ways to ruin your writing, but the most common offense is not knowing what you're trying to say in the first place.

Think back to Natalie's message to Miguel. What was she trying to achieve? Was she trying to be helpful, or did she just want to put pressure on Miguel? From Miguel's perspective, it seems like the latter. Message received loud and clear.

But let's assume Natalie was trying to be helpful. In that case, her message failed. The unintended pressure on Miguel created uncertainty throughout the company.

Remember our powerful purpose template from Chapter 1? Let's use it here to clarify Natalie's message:

As a [specific user], I want to [action] so that [definition of success] + [emotional and rational benefits].

- **Specific person:** Miguel (head of growth)
- **Action**: Share perspective on the lagging Net MRR
- **Success**: We reach our quarterly goal
- **Benefits (emotional)**: Have confidence and autonomy
- **Benefits (rational)**: Allow Natalie to clear any obstacles for him

Let's rewrite Natalie's email using her powerful purpose:

Miguel,

Would love your thoughts on the lagging Net MRR. Is there anything standing in our way from catching up and hitting our quarterly goal?

If not, you have my full confidence. If you do see any obstacles ahead, let me know and I'll work to get them out of your way. I'm available from 10–2 today if we need to gameplan.

Best,

Natalie

This new message has a clear purpose: to ensure the company hits their quarterly goal. Instead of applying undue pressure on Miguel, Natalie's message has a clear ask and is genuinely helpful. It promotes clarity and action, not uncertainty.

Leadership researcher and author Brené Brown has one of my favorite sayings about communication: "Clear is kind."

The burden of clarity is always on the communicator, not the person receiving the message. Before you send that next message, take a few moments to ensure you're crystal clear on its purpose.

Then it's time to write.

SIMPLIFY

How to Write More Clearly and Confidently

You could spend a lifetime studying the English language.

Or you could follow these eight simple rules of clear writing and get 95 percent of what you need.

Bookmark this page and keep it handy. These rules will save you time and countless hours of wasted energy:

1. KISS
2. Power of one
3. Frames of reference
4. Use active verbs
5. Make it personal
6. Write for skimmers
7. Deconstruct the writing process
8. Write fast, edit slow

Quick note: I call these *rules*, but like all rules in writing, they are merely suggestions. I recommend starting with the rules and breaking them as you get more comfortable and confident.

1. KISS: Keep it short and straightforward

Before he was a famous author, Ernest Hemingway was a newspaper reporter for the *The Kansas City Star*. At the *Star*, editors drilled Hemingway on the journalistic aesthetic of short, simple prose. He retained this style throughout his career, creating some of the most readable classic fiction available today.

Steve Jobs, a different kind of storyteller, was also known for his use of simple language and no-fluff messaging. Apple's technology was cutting edge, but Jobs's writing style hovered around a sixth- or seventh-grade reading level.

The lesson is simple: keep your writing short and straightforward. Clarity is far more valuable to your reader than a large vocabulary. Say what you mean and nothing more. Never use a longer word when a shorter word will do. Look for strings of words that can be replaced by a single, better word.

Short and straightforward writing is easier said than done. The challenge is that we tend to write whatever is on our minds, which is *not* always straightforward. The secret to KISS is not writing, but *rewriting* until you find the heart of what you're trying to say (more on this in Chapter 11: Never Skip Editing).

2. Power of one

The KISS principle extends beyond word choice. Keep

your sentences and paragraphs short and straightforward as well.

As a rule of thumb, share only one idea per sentence. When you're done with one idea, add a period and start your next sentence. Limit your use of compounds that combine two ideas into one sentence.

Remember this mantra: commas add complexity. More commas typically means more compound sentences. And compound sentences are harder to read.

We often create compound sentences because we're afraid to start a sentence with "And" or "But" or "Because." We were taught in school this was bad grammar. Starting a sentence with "But" may disappoint your high school English teacher. But the rest of us will be very happy.

I'll admit I break the comma rule a lot. Commas have their place in writing, especially when trying to create rhythm, but I always remove them when I can.

Power of one also applies to paragraphs. Keep paragraphs limited to just one idea. When you've made your point, move on to a new paragraph. Short chunks of text are much easier to read than large chunks, especially online.

And don't be afraid of the one-sentence paragraph.

3. Frames of reference

The legendary nonfiction writer John McPhee traveled the world to cover stories ranging from orange juice production in Florida to Wimbledon in Great Britain.

His topics were often obscure, so he'd connect with his audience by using their frames of reference. For example, when writing about an old and forgotten movie star, McPhee might describe him as "the Tom Cruise of his era." He called this technique *borrowed vividness.*

Frames of reference can bring color and comprehension to your writing, but only if they land. If you allude to something your reader doesn't know, it will have the opposite effect—you will lose their understanding and interest.

Frames of reference are just as important in business writing. Your reader's frames of reference include their industry knowledge, company culture, and your team's shared experiences.

But even your teammates have different frames of reference. Your marketing team has a different frame of reference than your development team. Your investors have a unique frame of reference as well.

Here's a simple example to illustrate my point: SQL. What does it mean to you?

If you have a sales or marketing background, SQL stands for Sales Qualified Lead. But if you're a developer, SQL is a scripting language.

Don't use acronyms that could alienate your audience or make them feel stupid for not knowing. But don't talk down to your audience, either. Explaining simple concepts to knowledgeable readers can make them resent you.

I once had a content marketing client who consulted enterprises on big data infrastructure. They hired us to write an ebook on big data architecture to use as marketing material. After the first draft, we got this harsh feedback from the client: "This ebook is too simplistic. Our customers are VPs and CTOs. This sounds like it was written for a freshman-level engineering course."

Had this version of the book gone out to my client's customers, they would have felt disrespected for being talked down to. Our client would have looked rude or unsophisticated. We cut out the basic definitions and dove deeper into the tech.

It's a delicate balance. Great writing will expand the reader's frame of reference without losing them entirely. But misjudging can lead to a complete breakdown of trust between parties.

When the message is particularly important, like a culturally sensitive topic, ask for feedback from people with personal experience. Seek to understand.

4. Use active verbs

I once had an English teacher tell me, "Never use passive verbs unless the subject is being murdered."

A little dramatic, but it's good writing advice.

As a leader, nothing kills your authority like passing blame. And that's exactly what passive verbs do.

- "This month's revenue goal *was stifled* by poor market conditions."
- "Shipping the software update *was delayed* by last-minute bugs."
- "The customer *was lost* in a price battle with our closest competitor."

Tell me, do these statements sound like leadership? Not at all. They actually sound like excuses.

Active verbs take responsibility.

- "*We missed* this month's revenue goals."
- "*We delayed* shipping due to last-minute bugs."
- "*I lost* the customer to a price battle."

Active verbs show you're tackling the problem head-on. That's great leadership—and great writing.

Next time you find yourself reaching for a passive phrase, stop to ask yourself why. Chances are you're trying to protect yourself. Active verbs force you to claim responsibility for a statement, whether it's good or bad.

Take responsibility. Use active verbs.

5. Make it personal

When one feels they occupy a higher station in life than their reader, one tends to write in a cold, third-person style like this.

Tell me, did you like reading that last sentence? Because I didn't enjoy writing it. Third-person writing removes *you* and *I* from the message and replaces us with labels like *people* or *they* or (the worst of them all) *one*. It feels bureaucratic and impersonal.

Use first person (I and we) and second person (you) language to make your writing more personal and conversational. Not just in emails, but in all of your writing. Did you notice I've used first- and second-person language throughout this book? You probably didn't until just now. And that's the point—it's completely natural.

Using first-person and second-person language doesn't just make your writing sound personal. It bonds you with the reader. "We have to solve this," is much more motivating than, "The company must solve this." Humans don't identify with terms like "people" or "the company." We respond to messages that are addressed to us directly.

In his groundbreaking behavioral psychology book, *Influence*, Robert Cialdini discusses the phenomenon of personalized language, but in a wildly different context. In emergency situations, studies have found that people won't take the necessary action to help unless they are addressed directly. Shouting, "Someone call an ambulance!" usually results in no one calling an ambulance. But pointing to someone and saying, "You there, in the green jacket, call an ambulance!" results in the correct action almost every time. The difference? Direct language removes uncertainty for the bystander. It's clear they must take action.

Remember this lesson while writing. If you want people to take action, address them directly.

There is only one instance where I prefer to use third person instead of addressing someone directly, and that's when I need to make it clear I'm talking to a specific group of people. This typically happens at the beginning of a piece of writing. I'll start by addressing my readers as, "SaaS founders" or "startup marketers" so that you know exactly who I'm writing for. Then I'll return to first- and second-person language.

6. Write for skimmers

Be honest, how often do you skim while reading? Even as

a writer and book publisher, I skim most things. There's just not enough time to read every word.

But when we write, we forget about the skimmer. We make the bold assumption that every reader will hang on to our every word. We bury the key points at the back end of long paragraphs. Then when the reader misses the key point, we blame it on them for not paying close attention.

Instead, imagine all of your readers are actually skimmers. How would you get the most important points across to them?

Here are a few ways to make your writing skimmable:

- Use section headers to summarize the piece
- Highlight, bold, and bullet-point your most important details.
- Make the first sentence of each paragraph the most important point.
- Save the least important information for the end (remember the inverted business pyramid).

Ironically, this will encourage some readers to dive deeper into your work. If they find your writing valuable after the first skim, they may go back and read it more thoroughly.

7. Deconstruct the writing process

Want to write more in less time? (Seriously, who doesn't?) The key is to deconstruct the writing process.

I struggled with daily writer's block for my first three years as content marketer. It got so bad I almost quit and went back to sales. Every blog post took three to four times longer than expected and I didn't know why.

The answer came after I hired my first freelance writer for WeContent. Working with someone else forced me to deconstruct my writing process for the first time. I broke it down into component parts and found what was tripping me up:

Writing isn't a singular activity. It actually consists of four separate stages, and each step requires a completely different mindset:

- Research = Curiosity
- Outline = Strategic thinking
- Write = Creativity
- Edit = Attention to detail

If you're struggling with writer's block like I was, chances are you're trying to combine two or more of these stages into one sitting. It's difficult to write (a creative act) when you're also trying to research and outline at the same time. It's even harder if you're trying to write and edit at once. The mental switching costs are heavy and can shut you down entirely.

To avoid writer's block and write more quickly, schedule time to complete each stage separately. Give your brain space to switch modes—even a five-minute break can be enough. The longer or more intensive the writing, the more time you should space between tasks. For example, when writing this book, I put two weeks in between writing the first draft and editing it.

My writing capacity literally tripled after deconstructing my writing process. I went from writing one blog post per week to at least three and sometimes more. Today I write about 1,200 words an hour, as long as my research and outline have been completed beforehand.

If you're in a hurry to write more, the key is to slow down. Separate each component part of writing and do one step at the time.

8. Write fast, edit slow

"The first draft of anything is shit," said Ernest Hemingway (allegedly).

Truth of source aside, the quote is a critical reminder for us: The enemy of good writing isn't bad writing. It's no writing at all.

Many writers are terrified of the blank page. They struggle to start because they're afraid of writing crap. They search and search and search for the perfect introduction, but the result is nothing at all.

Here's a secret all great writers know: Great writing isn't created in the first draft, or even the second. Great writing is made through editing.

And you can't edit a blank page.

So write your first draft quickly. Your first draft will be ugly and incoherent, and that's ok. All you need is words on a page to refine and mold.

Don't be fooled by the simplicity of clear writing. It never happens by accident. Like an iceberg, the real effort of clear communication is hidden below the surface. Even the most experienced communicators still work hard behind the scenes.

If at first you don't write clearly—and you won't—edit and edit again.

FREE TOOL #5 BONUS:
8 Rules of Writing Infographic

Great writing doesn't have to be hard. Simplify your writing quickly and easily with this free tool. Go to **www.greatfounderswrite.com/bonus**, enter your email, then click on "**8 Rules of Writing**" to get the infographic. Save or print this out as a useful reminder when writing.

NEVER SKIP EDITING

How to Mold Your Writing Into the Perfect Message

It took me years to get comfortable reading my own writing. It's a lot like hearing yourself talk on video. You feel exposed and a bit like a fraud.

Because of this, I would never edit my work. I would fly through the draft and hit send without a second thought. I told myself my writing sounded more natural this way. If "natural" meant sounding like an illiterate caveman, then I nailed it. In reality, I was just hurting my credibility and confidence.

My most embarrassing lapse in editing came shortly after college. I was in my first full-time job as a consultant for a non-profit. My boss knew I enjoyed writing, so he asked me to create a promotional flier for an upcoming event. I was excited about the project... so excited, I failed to edit. Over-confident and over-caffeinated, I breezed through the assignment and printed out the final version for my boss. He returned it fifteen minutes later with more red ink than I've ever seen. I made typos big and small. I even misspelled our organization's name!

I was completely embarrassed, but it taught me an invaluable lesson about writing. I pinned up that red-inked flier in my cubicle as a reminder to *always edit my work*.

Editing is more than just catching typos and grammatical errors. It's about saying what you mean in the clearest, most effective way. In this chapter, you'll learn my four-round editing process to help you nail every piece of writing.

I know what you're thinking. *Four rounds of editing? That's overkill. I'm a founder, not William Faulkner.*

But here's the thing: It's actually *easier* to edit four times than just once. This four-round edit will save you time in the long run. Let me explain why.

Much like deconstructing the writing process (see Chapter 10), the editing process can also be broken down into its component parts. Editing isn't just one task—it's four:

- Substance
- Style
- Voice
- Proofreading

First you edit for *substance*. Is your argument clear and compelling? Do you have your facts straight? Do you have the right stories and analogies to bring your piece to life?

Next you edit for *style*. Are you trying to sound formal or casual? Serious or funny? Expert or contrarian?

The third edit is for *voice*. Simply put, does your writing sound like it came from you and only you?

Finally, you proofread. This is where you check for grammar, punctuation, and spelling. (This is what most people think about when it comes to editing.)

It's really hard to edit for substance while proofreading at the same time. They require two different types of focus. By reviewing one layer at a time, you'll move smoothly and quickly through the editing process and feel more confident in the final product.

Let's look at each of the four edits more closely.

THE FOUR EDITS

Before we get started, here's a reminder from my editor: don't try to write and edit at the same time.

Write first, walk away from the draft, and *then* return to edit. Reviewing with fresh eyes will make a big difference. Even a minute of intentional breathing is enough to reset your brain to prepare for editing.

First edit: Substance

The first edit is all about the big picture. Forget grammar, punctuation, and word choice for now. Focus on the substance of your writing.

Here are the key questions to answer during the substance edit:

- Why am I writing this? (i.e., What is my purpose?)
- Who am I writing to and why should they care?
- Am I saying everything that needs to be said?
- Where are the holes in my logic?
- Are my stories interesting?
- What can I cut out?

Here's an example: Say you're writing a customer success playbook for your new customer support hire. You've written the first draft and you're now ready to edit.

The substance edit is to make sure the directions make sense. Read through your steps for providing excellent customer service—are they accurate? More importantly, are they *actionable* for someone new to the company? Did you provide enough context for your new employee to take over the job? Did you share *why* the role of customer success is vital to your company?

Think of the substance edit as your Minimal Viable Product, or MVP. Your writing won't be pretty, but it does the job you intended it to do.

With the bones of your writing in place, we'll start to clean it up in the second edit.

Second edit: Style

Like we learned in Chapter 4: Train Your Team for Success, *how* you deliver your content is just as important as *what* you deliver.

Think about style as the user interface of your writing. Maybe you prefer a clean and minimal design. Maybe you like something bold and dramatic. Some prefer a serious and professional style while others want to come off as irreverent and casual.

Writing style doesn't mean using frilly language and clever turns of phrase. It's simply *how* you deliver your content in a way that's most effective. The goal of the style edit is to make your writing clear *and* interesting.

You're no longer looking at the big picture here. During the style edit, you're reviewing each sentence on its own. Here are the key questions to ask yourself:

- How do I want my reader to describe me? (e.g., "The casual contrarian;" "The entertaining expert;" "The no-bull professional")
- How can I make each sentence more simple and straightforward?
- How can I make this phrase more clear (rather than clever)?
- Am I writing for the skimmers?
- Is my language personal?
- Am I using active verbs?

These questions map closely to the rules for clear writing from Chapter 10. Use that chapter as a guide during your style edit.

Let's go back to your customer success playbook. What vibe are you trying to give off? That of a no-bull professional or an entertaining expert? (In the case of this playbook, your writing style will likely impact the way your team interacts with customers, so be intentional.)

Can you simplify a sentence using a shorter word or phrase? Can you break up long sentences? Can you make a sentence more interesting with active verbs and personal language? Can you add headers, bulleted lists, and highlights to make the playbook skimmable?

Your second edit will take the most time, but this is where you really build communication leverage. Good style doesn't just make your writing easier to read—it builds credibility and trust with your readers.

Third edit: Voice

Voice is your personality in written form. Your writing should sound like it came from you and only you.

This is where many founders struggle. They feel the need to use big words and complicated phrases they would *never* say in real life. This makes their writing awkward and boring. It loses all personality.

How do you nail your writing voice so that it sounds like, well, *you*? Get ready to feel awkward —it's time to read your writing out loud.

The voice edit is done completely out loud (hence the name). Read your writing out loud to yourself or to another person. This is a research-backed technique to develop your writing voice. Studies have shown that humans are born with the ability to keep rhythm, and rhythm is a large part of what makes your voice unique.

As you read your work out loud, you'll discover clunky and unnatural sentences you'd never say during a conversation. You'll also catch issues with your pacing, where one paragraph abruptly ends while another drags on. You'll also notice missing words that your brain simply filled in while reading silently.

Reading your work out loud is like a superpower. It

will instantly enhance your writing voice with personality and rhythm.

Fourth edit: Proofread

The first three edits focused on the substance, style, and voice of your writing. Your work is now 90 percent done. But the last 10 percent takes your writing from good to great. This is the proofread.

Proofreading is the last bit of polish on your writing. This is where you check grammar, punctuation, spelling, and other rules you'd find in the Chicago or APA style guides. Skip this step at your own peril—a single misspelled word or run-on sentence can kill your credibility in some circles. It's not fair, but it's human nature to judge others on the tiniest mistakes.

I will not cover proofreading tips in detail here. There are many excellent books on the subject, including *Elements of Style* and the *Chicago Manual of Style*. But you don't even need to read those anymore—there are numerous proofreading tools that are effective and inexpensive. I recommend using Grammarly or the Hemmingway App to do your proofreading.

Remember: Proofreading should be your *last* round of editing you do, not the first (and definitely not the only.) If you find yourself making substance or style changes during the proofread, stop and restart the editing process. It will be worth it.

If you're not naturally confident in your writing, then congratulations: you're human. But this is not a life sentence. You can become a clear and confident writer by spending a little extra time on each piece. If writing is a muscle, this four-part editing process is your workout routine.

Apply daily for best results.

Now you know the secret of great writers: they are simply great editors. But there's one more trait that turns great writers—and great founders—into legendary ones.

That trait? The *courage* to show up, look themselves in the mirror, and do the right thing—even when it's hard.

That's next.

FREE TOOL #6 BONUS:
Editing Cheat Sheet

Never skip editing.

Go to **www.greatfounderswrite.com/bonus**, enter your email, then click on "Editing Cheat Sheet" to get the free tool. This cheat sheet will help you nail each round of editing so your message comes out perfect.

12

DESIGN FOR
EASY READING

*How to Format Your Writing To Reach More
People*

C hris Do is an accomplished graphic designer, entrepreneur, and teacher with more than one million YouTube subscribers. He's also the founder and CEO of The Futr, an online education platform with the mission of teaching one billion people how to make a living doing what they love.

One of Chris's most popular video series is where he critiques designs sent in from fans. Some of them are pretty rough. But no matter how bad a design is, he always follows the same thoughtful process.

First, he describes what he sees in the design. What's happening on the screen or page? His goal is to get a sense of the work as a whole before critiquing the parts.

Second, he thinks about how the design makes him

feel. This forces him to judge the piece emotionally before logic takes over.

Third, Chris identifies the strengths of the design. "Oh, I like this block of text," or, "The shape of the symbol fits nicely with the typography and works on a concept level."

Last but not least, Chris offers his suggestions for improvements. In logo design, the most common critiques are legibility, contrast, and creating a focal point.

Numerous studies have proven that good design increases user satisfaction and comprehension. Poorly designed things, from websites to office buildings, grate on us like sandpaper. They are literally exhausting to consume.

That's why the *design* of your writing is just as important as the content. Good design creates clarity. Before a reader reads a single word on this page, they judge the aesthetics of the work as a whole. We all judge books by their cover. The same is true for blog posts, emails, and investor memos.

Writing is your most powerful tool, but only if people read it.

We can learn a lot about writing from the way Chris critiques design work. Let's look at four design lessons to make your writing easier to read:

1. Give the reader direction

Good design gives your eyes a clear path to follow. We tend to notice bigger elements first, as well as elements in the forefront of the design. If you see eyes on a page, you'll naturally look to where they are looking. A web designer can use these techniques to guide a visitor directly to the call-to-action.

Writing has a natural starting point: the top left. But after that is a long, meandering path that few readers are willing to take. In the world of business writing, no one reads every word. That means you need to direct your reader to the most important information.

Most readers skim writing before deciding to read it more thoroughly. Readers will jump to the biggest elements first: your headers and subheaders. These are your directional arrows. Don't try to be clever—make your headers clear and descriptive.

Let's take this section as an example. This chapter is titled, "Design for Easy Reading." There's no question what you're going to learn here: writing lessons from the world of design.

Clever titles are more confusing than intriguing. Imagine if this chapter title was "Back to the drawing board." You'd have no idea what the chapter was about, and you'd probably skip it.

In business writing, it's better to be clear than clever. We're all too busy to play guessing games and risk wasting time on something irrelevant.

Good design provides clear direction.

2. Create focal points

Good design also creates clear focal points. Poor design has no focus, confusing the mind about where to look first. This is exhausting to the viewer, and most will simply give up trying.

Good writing also has focal points. The most important information should be easy to identify. Readers in a hurry should be able to jump to the most important text and get the gist of what you're saying. Poorly designed writing gives equal weight to every word. You may think every word is important, but your reader won't. If everything on the page seems important, readers will decide that nothing is important.

When speaking, we naturally emphasize the most important points. We enunciate, talk more loudly, and even repeat ourselves. You can do the same thing when you write.

Italicize for emphasis.

Bold or highlight the most important sentences.

Repeat yourself to create a rhythm of focal points.

Put the most important information at the beginning of a paragraph, not the end, and *definitely* not the middle (unless you want the reader to miss it).

You may have learned in school that such blunt writing tools were cheap tricks. But you're not just a writer; you're an entrepreneur. Forget "elegant" writing. Your goal should be ergonomic writing: useful, functional, and efficient.

Use every trick at your disposal. EVEN ALL CAPS.

But don't overdo it. Again, if every word seems important, nothing is.

3. Create white space

In design, what you *don't* see is just as important as what you do see.

White space is literally the space in between design elements. It's a critical piece in good design, and one that takes time to appreciate and master. Young designers often try to fit as much as possible on the page. Experienced designers know that white space is what makes their work stand out.

This principle is just as important in your writing.

Meredith Metzker, a journalist-turned-content marketer for SaaS startups, emphasizes the use of white space in her writing.

"Use the page like a designer uses white space," said Meredith. "Let your words breathe and stand out."

White space is an essential counterpart to focal points. Without white space, you'll have a wall of impenetrable text. Researchers have found that a lack of white space (specifically the use of small margins and tight line spacing) can lower reading comprehension. If you need proof of this for yourself, just try reading a research paper in an academic journal—most will make your eyes bleed.

Creating white space starts with your sentences and paragraphs. Keep your paragraphs short—typically no more than three sentences.

And dare to use single-sentence paragraphs to break up the monotony.

Next, use bulleted lists whenever possible. These create blocks of lateral white space that give your writing a nice shape.

Finally, take time to develop the right message so that you can say less.

Improve your emails with white space

White space is especially important in emails, which is where you'll probably conduct the majority of your writing. White space makes emails more clear, focused, and effective.

In my opinion, no one writes a more clear and effective email than Trish Bertuzzi. Trish is the author of *The Sales Development Playbook*. She's mastered the art of writing sales emails that convert. White space is a fundamental element of her success.

Trish is a proponent of short emails that take the shape of a capital F.

The first paragraph is the longest, and they get shorter and shorter down the email. This pattern creates a natural "funnel" design—a clear direction for the reader.

Here's an example of a sales email I used when building WeContent, my content marketing agency:

Hey Lauren,

I really liked [Company]'s blog post on switching big data platforms from Amazon AWS to Snowflake. But I noticed it's the only article you've written this quarter.

Did you know companies that publish more than one blog post per week see a 10× the return on their content marketing efforts?

We help companies like [Company] publish more content for a flat fee.

If interested, let's talk. Here's my calendar link.

Cheers,

Ben Putano

Notice this message has more white space around the

call-to-action at the end of the email. My goal is to funnel attention to the calendar link. This email performed very well for me (and led to the training debacle I shared in Chapter 4).

4. Design for clarity

Chris Do's biggest pet peeve when critiquing design: Legibility!

Amateur designers often sacrifice readability for style. This type of design serves no one but the designer. "Legibility should supersede every other consideration," said Chris.

For writers, this obviously means to avoid illegible fonts. But it's also a reminder to prioritize clarity over style. And as we've seen, clarity is more than the words you choose—it's about giving your reader a clear direction through good design. Never assume your words will be read, even when writing to a captive audience like your employees. Your reader's attention is *always* earned.

Design your writing to be clear, interesting, and easy to read. Then watch your impact and influence soar.

PART 4:
WRITE WITH COURAGE

"It is not the critic who counts; not the man who points out how the strong man stumbles, or where the doer of deeds could have done them better. The credit belongs to the man who is actually in the arena, whose face is marred by dust and sweat and blood; who strives valiantly; who errs, who comes short again and again; who spends himself in a worthy cause; who at the best knows in the end the triumph of high achievement, and who at the worst, if he fails, at least fails while daring greatly, so that his place shall never be with those cold and timid souls who neither know victory nor defeat."

—THEODORE ROOSEVELT

13

LEAD FROM THE FRONT

How to Deliver Bad News, Take a Stand, and Do the Right Thing During Crisis

Over ten hours had passed when Robinhood cofounder and CEO, Vlad Tenev, finally broke his silence. By then he had become the most hated man on Wall Street. Maybe in all of America.

Earlier that day, on January 28, 2021, Tenev and his executive team made the decision to freeze the buying of GameStop stock ($GME), along with several other stocks that were targets of a historic short squeeze.

Unlike past short squeezes, which were weapons of the financial elite, this one was orchestrated and led by regular people. Retail investors met and rallied through a Reddit forum called WallStreetBets (WSB). Soon, the entire world was in on the action, from nurses in L.A. to Elon Musk. In just a matter of months, $GME rose from

$5 per share to almost $500. The frenzy pushed hedge fund shorters to the edge of bankruptcy, costing them billions of dollars in the process.

This was exactly the type of revolution you'd think Robinhood would welcome. After all, Tenev built Robinhood with a mission to democratize finance for all. Yet at the peak of the $GME's rise, when it looked like nothing could slow the stock down, the investment platform halted trading. It was a death blow to the WSB short-squeezers.

In hindsight, Robinhood's action were completely justified. But their poor communication during the chaos turned them into villains. Alex Lieberman, co-founder of Morning Brew, summed up the destruction best on Twitter:

"Robinhood is officially a case study in the fragility of brand. It took them 7 years to build up confidence in their platform. It took them 1 day to switch from 'by the people' to 'against the people.'"

Courage—or the lack thereof—is revealed in crisis.

Robinhood was put in an impossible position. But the real damage was self-inflicted. Tenev and his team showed no courage when addressing their customers, destroying all the goodwill they had worked so hard to build up. They may never fully recover from the fallout of January 28, 2021.

When people are turning to you for answers, how will you respond? We can look at Robinhood as an example of what *not* to do when courageous leadership—and writing—is required.

Writing with courage can be distilled into 7 principles:

1. Be visible
2. Be direct
3. Be honest
4. Be helpful
5. Be accountable
6. Be human
7. Share next steps

Robinhood broke them all.

Let's look at each one and see what we can learn.

1. BE VISIBLE

Tenev's first mistake was simply not showing up when people needed him. The ten hours it took for him to address Robinhood's decision to freeze $GME trading is inexcusable. In that time, wild conspiracy theories raged all over the internet.

An internet sleuth discovered that one of Robinhood's largest investors, D1 Capital, held a large short position against GameStop. The fund had lost 20 percent of its value in a matter of weeks. Was this why Robinhood delisted GameStop?

Later, an even more damning fact surfaced: Robinhood's largest enterprise customer, Citadel Securities, had recently invested in a hedge fund who was on the verge of bankruptcy from the GameStop short squeeze. Just a coincidence? Or was Robinhood forced to take action by a powerful institution?

The truth was much more boring. Robinhood faced a compliance issue that threatened to shut down the entire platform. While trading on Robinhood appears instant, transactions take up to two days to officially process. A rule called T-2 requires Robinhood to keep cash on hand to cover those trades until they're completed. The GameStop frenzy pushed Robinhood's cash requirements to a hundred times their normal levels. On January 28, they had just five hours to either come up with the cash or get shut down by the government. By freezing $GME and other rallying stocks, they were able to lower their cash requirements and keep the platform afloat.

But no one knew this until Tenev posted a Twitter thread about it—ten hours after the freeze occurred. Instead of being up front with customers, Tenev disappeared, which is suspicious in itself. The void of information was filled by a public desperate for answers.

The first rule of communication during a crisis: Be visible. Vlad Tenev was not.

2. BE DIRECT

During moments of crisis, be direct. Skip the formalities and business-speak. Give people the information they need.

Vlad Tenev should have been on the front lines communicating with customers during the GameStop crisis. Instead, he directed his comms team to release an anemic blog post titled, "Keeping Customers Informed Through Market Volatility."

The first problem with the article is the title. It's as generic and bureaucratic as you can get. Using the phrase "market volatility" on the day of the largest short squeeze in history isn't just an understatement—it's misleading. Customers seeking answers on Robinhood's blog overlooked the post because it didn't directly address GameStop.

The blog post's problems continued in the first paragraph. Instead of addressing the $GME freeze outright, Robinhood led with their mission statement. Then they said how proud they were of themselves:

> *Our mission at Robinhood is to democratize finance for all. We're proud to have created a platform that has helped everyday people, from all backgrounds, shape their financial futures and invest for the long term.*

In a moment when users have tens of thousands of dollars or more at stake, no one cares about your mission statement or your past success. They only care about one thing: their money.

When Robinhood did finally address the short squeeze, they still refused to be direct with customers:

> *In light of recent volatility, we restricted transactions for **certain securities** to position closing only. You can see the latest here [Link to blog]. We also raised margin requirements for certain securities. (Emphasis mine)*

Not once did Robinhood mention the GameStop by name in the post. Users had to visit a different blog post to see the list of restricted stocks. At that point, a concerned customer could only assume Robinhood was being opaque on purpose.

3. BE HONEST

During a crisis, any whiff of dishonesty will shatter your trust with customers.

Robinhood never outright lied during the GameStop short squeeze, but they withheld crucial information from the public for an entire trading day— specifically, the reason *why* they froze $GME. This lack of transparency was dishonest in its own way.

Tenev should have immediately shared everything he knew with the public using a tried-and-true phrase from the history of crisis communication, "Here's what we know." There was no benefit of withholding information if they had nothing to hide.

As a leader, you won't have all the answers during a crisis, but that's no excuse for not sharing what you know. Customers don't need perfect information, but they need *something*.

Tenev's integrity was called into question because it took so long for him to respond. The longer it takes to tell the truth, the less likely people are to believe you.

4. BE HELPFUL

The "fog of war" is a military term that describes the confusion and chaos that covers a battlefield. It can be blinding and disorienting. During times of crisis, when the fog of war is thick, leaders need to help their people reach the other side in one piece.

Robinhood again failed this test in spectacular fashion. Not only did they fail to provide a helpful explanation for freezing $GME, but they sent readers on a wild goose chase to find their own answers.

Here's a paragraph from Robinhood's blog post on January 28:

> *Amid significant market volatility, it's important as ever that we help customers stay informed.* **That's why we're committed to providing people with educational resources. We recently revamped and expanded RobinhoodLearn** *to help people take advantage of the hundreds of financial resources we offer and educate themselves, including how to make sense of a volatile market.* (Emphasis mine)

When you click the link to go to Robinhood Learn, it doesn't go to a specific article, but straight to the resource center homepage. The first post is titled, "Investing 101."

Insulting.

In this case, Robinhood was less than helpful. They were condescending. They might as well have said, "You clearly don't understand how the stock market works. Let us enlighten you."

The next day, on January 29, the comms team published another blog post, this one about the financial mechanics behind trading. Again, they failed to provide a helpful explanation for the $GME freeze. Buried three-quarters down the page, in the back half of an unassuming paragraph, was this jargon-filled statement:

> *This week alone, our clearinghouse-mandated deposit requirements related to equities increased ten-fold. And that's what led us to put temporary buying restrictions*

*in place on a small number of securities that the
clearinghouses had raised their deposit requirements on.*

(Note: During a crisis, it's critical to write using the
inverted business pyramid we discussed in Chapter 2.)

It wasn't until three full days later, on February 1, that
Robinhood finally provided a simple, clear explanation
for their actions:

*Simply put, Robinhood limited buying in volatile
securities to ensure it complied with deposit regulations.*

But by that point, the Robinhood's reputation was
destroyed. The opportunity to help their users through
the crisis had long passed.

5. BE ACCOUNTABLE

Robinhood's decision to freeze $GME turned a chaotic
situation into a crisis. Yet the company never took
responsibility for their role.

Without Robinhood's zero-commission trading tool,
the short squeeze would have never been possible. Did
they ever consider something like this could happen? It's
not like they didn't have warning signs—GME trade volume rose rapidly throughout the month of January,
which meant Robinhood needed more and more cash on
hand to cover deposits. In hindsight, couldn't they have
been more prepared?

Worst of all, Robinhood never took responsibility for
fixing the situation. After announcing the stock freeze,
they made no indication they were working to unfreeze

them. Instead, they seemed to blame their customers for the freeze:

> We're determined to provide new and experienced investors with the tools and resources to **help them invest responsibly for their long-term financial futures.** (Emphasis mine)

They might as well have said, "You'll get your stocks back when you're responsible enough to trade them."

As a founder, the buck stops with you. It's your responsibility to foresee and avoid a crisis. When that's not possible, it's your job to fix it.

Be accountable.

6. BE HUMAN

All of Robinhood's missteps were exacerbated by communication that sounded like it was written by legal. (It probably was.) Here's one of the more obtuse statements from Tenev's Twitter thread on January 28:

> As a brokerage firm, Robinhood has many financial requirements, including SEC net capital obligations and clearinghouse deposits. Some of these requirements fluctuate based on volatility in the markets and can be substantial in the current environment.

Using legal-approved jargon like "volatility" and "current environment" raised more questions than answers for Robinhood users. Tenev's worst offense was refusing to mention the stock at the heart of the entire crisis,

GameStop, as if uttering the name would open them up to legal action.

As a platform for the people, Robinhood failed to communicate like a real person. Instead they opted to hide behind corporate jargon and legal-washed messaging.

7. PROVIDE NEXT STEPS

Desperate Robinhood customers needed answers about their $GME stock. When would the freeze be lifted? What would happen next?

Ten hours after the freeze, Tenev offered some painfully vague next steps in his Twitter thread. He said Robinhood would open up limited sales of $GME and other stocks the next day. But what did "limited" mean, exactly? And could Robinhood freeze the stock again?

Robinhood failed to give any more direction to their customers or the public. This led anxious users to seek out new leaders—folks like Dave Portnoy, the founder of Barstool Sports, who called for the imprisonment of Tenev and his hedge fund overlords on social media. His position may have been extreme, but at least he gave his followers hope for a resolution.

At the end of his Twitter thread, Vlad Tenev offered an "apology" of sorts:

> *"We cannot control... **the lightning-fast spread of information** and misinformation that takes place on social media, and for that I am incredibly sorry to our customers and staff for this."* (Emphasis mine)

That statement is a perfect summary of everything that Robinhood did wrong on January 28.

Tenev and his team lacked urgency to help their customers manage the crisis. They failed to share visible, direct, honest, and helpful information that the public desperately craved. After ten hours of silence, when conspiracy theories filled the void, they blamed "the lightning-fast spread of information" and said it was out of their control.

Robinhood failed to lead—and write—with courage.

Could things have been different?

WHAT COURAGEOUS COMMUNICATION LOOKS LIKE

We know what Robinhood did wrong, but how should they have responded instead? Luckily, we don't need to hypothesize.

Public.com is a commission-free trading platform, just like Robinhood. On January 28, they were also forced to freeze $GME and other stocks during the squeeze. But their response to the crisis couldn't have been more different.

From their very first message, Public.com's response to the GameStop freeze was the exact opposite of Robinhood's.

In short, it was courageous.

Here's Public.com's Tweet announcing the freezing of GME and other stocks:

Our clearing firm, Apex Holdings, has decided to halt the buying of $KOSS, $GME, and $AMC. We are in *close contact with the firm and will make sure to keep our members informed as soon as we get updates.*

We disagree with this decision and are working hard for our members to resolve the issue. We'll provide updates here as they happen.

This one Tweet alone nails every rule of good crisis communication.

- **Be visible**—This message was sent immediately upon freezing the stocks. Public.com's Twitter account was active throughout the day.

- **Be direct**—Public.com listed the affected stocks in their Tweet, unlike Robinhood, who refused to mention $GME outright.

- **Be honest**—Public.com shared everything they knew about the situation with their customers, including the fact it was their clearing firm that forced them to halt trading.

- **Be helpful**—Public.com promised to keep their members informed.

- **Be accountable**—It wasn't Public.com's fault that trading was halted, but they took responsibility for resolving the issue as quickly as possible.

- **Be human**—Public.com publicly disagreed with the decision to halt stocks, a decision that actively hurt their customers. You can sense their urgency in this Tweet. They didn't just recite their mission statement—they were living it.

- **Provide next steps**—Public.com said they were working closely with their clearing firm and promised updates to their customers.

But here's the most amazing part of Public.com's response on January 28:

Less than ten hours after freezing the stocks—and a full forty-five minutes *before* Vlad Tenev's Twitter thread explanation—Public.com resolved the issue with their clearing firm and unfroze the stocks.

Courageous writing leads to courageous action.

Public.com turned the GameStop crisis into a golden opportunity. In February 2021, the company raised $220 million in venture capital to become the *real* trading platform for the people. In the year that followed the GameStop debacle, Public's user base grew 700 percent.

Robinhood, meanwhile, has struggled to rebuild trust in their platform. The company went public in July 2021, but their stock has since fallen more than 80 percent. With little brand loyalty to buoy them, they are now a prime target for a corporate takeover.

Great founders say what needs to be said, even when it's hard. They choose to be visible, direct, honest, accountable, helpful, and human in their communications. They don't let a crisis overtake them. They step up and lead.

The GameStop short squeeze gave us two excellent case studies to learn from. One was an industry leader whose lack of courage may still cost them everything. The other was a contender who turned the crisis into a massive win by putting their customers first.

The choice is yours. Will you lead from the front?

BUILD YOUR AUDIENCE

How to Attract the Right Followers to Grow Your Business

B uilding an online audience requires a different kind of courage than leading through a crisis. You're *choosing* to put yourself out there, even when you'd rather be anywhere else.

And for those with the courage to build an audience, the payoff is massive.

Naval Ravikant, co-founder of AngelList, believes media is the most powerful form of leverage today (along with software). That's because, unlike capital and labor, media is *permissionless* leverage.

Here's an excerpt from *The Almanack of Naval Ravikant* by Eric Jorgenson:

> *"[Media and code] don't require somebody else's permission for you to use them or succeed. For labor leverage, somebody has to decide to follow you. For capital leverage, somebody has to give you money to invest or to turn into a product.*
>
> *Coding, writing books, recording podcasts, tweets, YouTubing—these kinds of things are permissionless. You don't need anyone's permission to do them, and that's why they are very egalitarian. They're the great equalizers of leverage."*

We see examples of permissionless leverage everywhere online today.

In 2021, Shaan Puri, co-founder of *The Hustle* and *Milk Road*, set out to raise a $1 million rolling venture fund in twenty-one days. He sent a single Tweet to his (at the time) 100,000 followers and raised $1.5 million... *in just five days.* Meanwhile, eighteen-year-old Charli D'Amelio has built a business empire and launched her acting career by amassing a TikTok audience of over 100 million followers.

But many founders don't want to build a big personal audience. They feel like self-promotion is inauthentic and spammy. They hate being in the spotlight and have no interest in becoming a "thought leader." And the idea of spending 24/7 on social media sounds like a living hell.

If you're nodding your head in agreement to the statements above, this chapter is for you.

Because here's the truth: You don't need a massive online audience to grow your business. You just need the *right* audience—an audience of ideal customers and superfans who will promote and pay for your work.

The size of your audience is irrelevant. You don't need a million followers, or 100,000 followers, or even 10,000 followers. Most important is *who* you're attracting and *why*.

WHEN A BIGGER AUDIENCE ISN'T BETTER

Jay Acunzo is a father, author, keynote speaker, podcaster, and one of the best B2B storytellers in the business. Brands pay him $2,500 an hour to develop content that resonates with their audiences.

But Acunzo's personal audience? Not as big as you might think. At around 20,000 Twitter followers, he's a relatively small fish in the world of B2B marketing. This is by choice.

"I have a small but passionate, long-lasting, and very loyal audience from a lot of premium brands. So I can charge higher amounts for what I offer," said Acunzo on an episode of the *Creative Elements* podcast with Jay Clouse.

Acunzo's high-value audience allows him to charge more while earning higher profit margins and working with fewer people. He didn't build a bigger audience, but a better one. That's the definition of leverage.

Acunzo uses an analogy to illustrate his audience-building strategy:

> *Are you building a Toyota audience or a Tesla audience?*

Toyota is a car for just about everyone. It's safe, reliable, and relatively affordable. Because of this, Toyota has a massive global audience. But a car for everyone is, by nature, average. No one will fault you for buying a Toyota, but no one is gawking at your new whip, either. Tesla, on the other hand, is distinctly *not* for everyone. Their first model was a $100,000 electric sports car—it was exciting, expensive, and *exclusive*. Tesla created a premium product for the elite few, and they built a rabid fanbase in the process.

There's nothing wrong with building a Toyota audience. Toyota is one of the world's most popular brands for a reason. But building a global audience doesn't work for every type of business. Acunzo's consulting and speaking business is better served by a Tesla audience. He sells high-value products and services to deep-pocketed customers who love his work. He doesn't need a large audience to succeed—just a passionate one.

But the greatest advantage to building a Tesla audience is not the raving fan base, or even the higher profit margins that come from charging premium prices. It's the freedom to *choose* how and when to grow.

Thanks to a quirk in buyer psychology, being exclusive makes you even more desirable to the masses. Millions of people want a Tesla who can't afford it. Tens of thousands of marketers and entrepreneurs want an hour of Acunzo's time but could never afford his rate. Your exclusivity creates pent-up demand. Your brand becomes *aspirational*.

With an aspirational brand and pent-up demand, you have the choice to "move downstream" by offering lower-priced products. This is exactly what Tesla has done with the Model 3, a car similarly priced to a brand-new Toyota Camry. But the psychology doesn't work in reverse. "Toyota couldn't just move upstream," said Acunzo. "They had to create an entirely new premium brand: Lexus."

Acuzno has also moved downstream to tap into pent-up demand. He's launched courses and communities that cost a fraction of his hourly consulting rate. He also creates loads of free content through his podcast, newsletter, blog, and social channels. This free content attracts a younger, less-affluent fan base that may one day earn enough to pay Jay's premium rate—or not. Either way, thanks to his high-paying customers, everybody wins.

"I like to tell my subscribers: when a few benefit, we all benefit."

If you're selling high-value goods or services, you don't want to build a large following of casual onlookers. You want a small but fiercely passionate audience of fans who can afford what you do—or aspire to do so. In other words, you want to build a Tesla audience. This will give you the option to stay exclusive—earning more profit from fewer customers—or go downstream to tap into pent-up demand.

Media may be the new leverage, but a bigger audience is not always better. Let's look at exactly how to build a high-value audience for your business.

FIVE PRINCIPLES FOR BUILDING A HIGH-VALUE AUDIENCE OF ANY SIZE

Building a high-value audience starts with creating high-value content.

This is not a lesson in going viral or hacking social media algorithms. Those tactics change constantly and are not entirely in your control anyway. Instead, I'm going to share five principles for building an engaged, passionate following of any size. These principles haven't changed in millennia, and they aren't likely to change anytime soon.

Let's dive in.

1. Set the right goals

The first step to building an engaged audience is knowing why you're building one in the first place.

Jay Acunzo knows exactly why he's building an online audience: to support his high-ticket consulting and speaking business. This is one reason why he chose to start a podcast—a terrible channel if your goal is to build a large audience, but excellent for building deep relationships with your listeners.

Amanda Natividad also has clear goals. As the VP of Marketing at SparkToro, an audience research startup, her Twitter following has recently ballooned to over 100,000 followers. But building a large audience was never the point. "I don't want to be famous or *go viral*," she told me. "I just want my ideas to resonate in my industry."

Natividad thinks about audience-building as a tool. She calls it *networking at scale.* Her audience gives her the type of leverage that Naval alluded to: a marketplace for her ideas, businesses, and side-projects.

But goal-setting is a tradeoff. Any goal will take time and energy away from your other priorities. Whether you want to build a Toyota audience or Tesla audience, your efforts need to fit in with the rest of your work and personal life.

To set the right goals for your audience-building aspirations, I use a technique called *ecological goal-setting*. See Chapter 15 for the full exercise.

2. Make your customer the hero

Everyone lives as the main character of their own story. Remember this as you set out to build an audience. *You* are not the hero—your customer is.

Your role is to guide them on their journey.

The Hero's Journey is a story as old as time. It's the ultimate saga of human trial and triumph. Any time we find ourselves wanting, striving, succeeding, *or* failing, we're following in the footsteps of our favorite heroes: Hercules, Joan of Arc, Luke Skywalker, Usain Bolt, and Queen Elsa.

Many companies use the Hero's Journey to connect with potential customers. One of the best modern examples is Nike, the brand that promises to "Bring inspiration and innovation to every athlete* in the world (*If you have a body, you are an athlete.)" Nike supports athletes with equipment, clothing, and inspiration to do what they do best. They make their customers the hero—those of us who strive to be like Serena Williams or Michael Jordan.

But not everyone sees themselves as a hero. Some people want to be rebels. Others want to be adventurers. Again, brands play the role of the guide: Harley Davidson and Vans help their customers feel like outlaws. Patagonia and Red Bull fuel our epic journeys.

Traditional marketing logic says to put your brand at the center of the story:

"Recommended by nine out of ten dentists."

"Choosy moms choose Jif."

"The World's Cheapest Car."

But today's best brands teach us a different lesson: Make your customer the hero, rebel, or adventurer of their own story. Your job is to guide them along the way.

Map out your customer journey

So how do you make your customer the main character of your story?

First you need to know what their unique journey looks like. Then you need to create content that serves as a guidebook for them along the way.

During my days at WeContent, we developed a tool to help companies tell more customer-centric stories: *The Heroic Customer Story (HCS) framework.* The HCS not only helps you build empathy for your customer, but identify content ideas for every part of their journey.

Spend time answering each question of the HCS in detail. By the end, you'll have dozens of high-value content ideas that have a direct impact on your customer's life.

1. The Hero
    ◦ What's your customer's name?
    ◦ Do they see themselves as the hero, rebel, outlaw, adventurer, caregiver, or something else?
    ◦ What is their current status quo like?

2. Aspirations
   - What do they want out of life?
   - What do they need?

3. Challenges
   - What stands in their way from living the life they want?

4. Call to action
   - Who, or what, finally motivates them to change the status quo and seek out their aspirations?

5. They meet a guide (you or your brand)
   - Why do you want to help? (Consider your mission and business goals)
   - Why should they trust you?

6. Who paints a vision
   - What could life really look like for your hero?

7. Gives them tools and a plan
   - How can you help your hero live their best life?

8. Hero faces obstacles
   - What challenges will the hero face along the way?
   - What external challenges stand in their way?
   - What internal beliefs must they battle?

9. But achieves victory
   - What does "success" look like for your customer?
   - How will you know when they've achieved it?
   - What will success hear, sound, and feel like?

10. And transforms along the way
    - Who will your customer become on their journey?

The Heroic Customer Story aims to plant you in the life of your customers for the long haul. Paint the vision, help them along their journey, and watch them transform into the people they were meant to be.

One last thing to keep in mind: who you're *not* writing for is just as important as who you are writing for. Many people (including myself) naturally aim to please everybody. This is a bad habit that can make our writing boring and average.

Take a moment to describe exactly who you're not trying to serve in your writing. This will give your work a distinct edge—a line that differentiates your community from everyone else.

Don't be offensive, but don't be afraid to be an acquired taste, either.

3. Position yourself — Part 1: own a niche

With your Heroic Customer Story mapped out, now it's time to talk about *you*. How will you stand out from the crowd?

It's not just about *what* you write about, but *how* you do it.

When it comes to positioning, there are two schools of thought: Owning a niche, and finding your key differentiators.

A niche is an untapped segment of your market that is currently underserved by the competition. This path is getting more and more difficult due to the explosion of competition in virtually every industry, but it can be very lucrative. To find an unoccupied niche, you have two options:

Split an existing niche into an even more specific sub-segment

For example, if you're building a CRM for small real estate investors, you're already facing fierce competition. But what if you niched down to female investors just getting into real estate? In a male-dominated industry, this could be a lucrative niche. Ellevest has carved out a similar position in ETF investing.

Create a new category

Category creation is the process of creating a brand-new class of product or way of doing business. For individuals, category creation could also mean coining a term for the type of work you do. Nicolas Cole, for example, coined the term "digital writer" for someone who writes online to grow their audience. Being a category creator can be highly lucrative but challenging. First, you need to create a truly different product or experience. Second, you need to educate your audience on what this new category is and why they should care.

The biggest benefit to owning a niche is the opportunity for rapid growth. If you find a truly untapped market—especially one that's highly motivated and interconnected—you can become *the* go-to resource for that audience. Owning a niche makes you immediately recognizable and more memorable in a crowded market.

But there are downsides to owning a niche. The biggest drawback is boxing yourself into a highly specific category. Owning a niche requires you to stay obsessively on-topic. This is constraining for anyone who wants to explore multiple interests. It also caps your potential growth to the size of your niche unless you choose to branch out. Many individuals and brands have successfully grown out of their niche, but you risk losing your most fervent audience members by doing so.

4. Position yourself — Part 2: key differentiators

So what's the alternative to owning a niche? Find your key differentiators.

"I don't think you have to double down on a niche in order to grow," Amanda Natividad told me. "If you focus on your key differentiators instead, you'll be able to grow your audience in a healthier way."

Finding your key differentiators is a little less cut-and-try than owning a niche. Simply put, your key differentiators are what make you different and better for your target audience. This could include a single factor like price, or a combination of hard and soft traits like your business model, values, tone of voice, or customer service.

It can be slower to build an audience based on your key differentiators than by owning a niche. But the benefit is an audience who follows you for *you*, not your category.

"Focusing on your key differentiators will lead you to developing true fans—people who follow you and care about what you have to say based on the way you think," said Natividad.

To find your key differentiators, ask yourself these four questions:

What am I *really* good at?

Don't just think about your marketable skills, but your personality and soft skills as well.

For example, Natividad is an expert in content marketing—she's done it for eight years for some of the biggest brands in the world. But she's also a professionally trained chef and has a knack for making people feel seen and appreciated. This is a unique and powerful triad of skills.

Think about the compliments you get, what people pay you to do, and the traits that make you, *you*.

What am I interested in?

If you're a human being, your interests probably extend beyond your work (sorry, robots).

Your mix of interests can be one of your key differentiators. I write and publish books for entrepreneurs, but I also love travel, urban planning, architecture, and playing ultimate frisbee. These aren't passive interests, either. I learn important lessons about life and work from these extracurriculars.

Natividad is obviously interested in content marketing, but she also loves to share original recipes for food and cocktails. And as a mother, she also shares occasional misadventures of family life.

What does my audience want or need?

By this point you should have a clear idea what your audience is looking for. Refer to your Heroic Customer Story:

- What do your customers want out of life?
- What do they *need*?
- What stands in their way from living the life they want?
- Who do they want to become?

How can I deliver differently?

Owning a niche is about *what* you do. Your key differentiators focus on *how* you do it. That makes a huge difference for your audience.

Steph Smith, an author and podcast host at Andreeson Horowitz, said in an interview with Growth Machine:

> *"Rather than focus on your end product or service—your 'what'—focus on your how: how you, and only you, can deliver this product differently.*
>
> *Will you bring a sense of humor to an otherwise stale industry? Could you provide short, easy-to-digest snippets of information? Can you design infographics that help break down complex topics?"*

How you deliver your products, services, and ideas is just as important as *what* you deliver. Don't underestimate the power of being different.

Your key differentiators live at the intersection of these four questions. Take stock of all the things that separate you from your competitors, then combine them in a unique way. Don't look for validation from your industry—if you do it right, your approach will be unlike anything else. And that's exactly what you want.

"If you can see your path laid out in front of you step by step, you know it's not your path," said Joseph Campbell, author of *The Hero with a Thousand Faces*. "Your own path you make with every step you take. That's why it's your path."

Be bold. Be different. Be relentlessly *you*.

5. Show up consistently

The number one reason why founders fail to build an audience is that they give up before they ever really get started.

Building an audience takes time. Starting and stopping after three months will look like a failure, but you haven't even left the starting gate. Prepare to commit to twelve to eighteen months of consistent writing.

But the exact definition of consistency is different for everyone. Social media rewards people who show up daily, but it's more important to pick a cadence that works for you. Don't push out C-grade content just to say you did it.

Consistency is the most reliable way to improve your skills as a writer and build momentum with your audience. Start by blocking time on your calendar for content creation. This could be twenty minutes, an hour, or even a few hours every week. Protect this time as an investment in your future. Every piece of writing is another degree of leverage for your business.

Refine your content strategy over time by seeing what performs and what doesn't. If one newsletter outperforms the others by two or three times, take that as a sign of a topic your audience is interested in. Explore that topic deeper to see if you can double down on your success. At the same time, watch for topics that fall flat. Keep tweaking your messaging until you get the response you want or move on to topics with higher engagement.

Consistency is the only thing you can't fake. If your goal is to build an audience, be nothing if not consistent.

LAST THING: BUILD RELATIONSHIPS WITH YOUR AUDIENCE

As a writer and entrepreneur, the thing I value most is the people I've met on my journey.

Building an audience can quickly become a soulless numbers game if you forget about the people on the other side. Take time to start one-on-one conversations and build actual relationships with others. If you're on Twitter, DM someone who regularly comments on your posts. Ask them about their goals and how you can help. Jump on a call with an email subscriber who opens every one of your newsletters. Where do they live? What do they do in their free time? What obstacles stand in their way?

Building relationships is good for the soul and good for business. It's very difficult to quit products or services when you've had a personal conversation with the founder. The more time you spend building relationships, the more fervent your audience will become.

Two people stand out to me as excellent relationship-builders: Mac Conwell and Arvid Kahl. You know Mac from Chapter 8: Nurture Key Relationships. He regularly takes over two hundred phone calls a month with founders, limited partners, and aspiring entrepreneurs looking for advice. Mac's spotlight has grown because of the personal relationships he's built.

Arvid Kahl is also generous with his time. After selling a SaaS business, Arvid began writing books for boot-strapped founders. He found success by writing in public and asking his audience to help. He's built relationships that extend far beyond one book or business.

Don't measure your success by the size of your audience. Measure it by the quality of relationships you build. If you can say you've met one person who has changed your life for the better, I would call that a victory. Now you're playing with house money.

It's time to put yourself in the spotlight.

PRACTICE PRACTICE PRACTICE

How to Master The Craft of Writing

I n architecture, a keystone is a wedge-shaped rock that sits at the pinnacle of an archway. It balances the forces of the opposing sides of the arch, holding the structure together with surprising strength. In fact, the more weight you put on top of the keystone, the stronger the arch becomes.

Entrepreneurship is a lot like building an arch. The keystone is your writing routine.

Good writing strengthens every other part of your business, from decision-making to marketing. It's vital for keeping opposing forces and emotions in balance. Without a writing routine, your archway is more likely to topple.

My friend and fellow entrepreneur Andy Ellwood has maintained a writing routine for over fifteen years.

Through journals and blogging, Andy has used writing as a tool to build a successful career at some of the fastest-growing startups in tech. It's also helped him navigate personal challenges and reinvent himself several times over.

My own writing routine has evolved over time. Although I write every day now, this wasn't always the case. I started with occasional journaling, a blog post here and there, and writing notes to myself on my phone. I wasn't very consistent, but I kept at it until I reached a point in my life where I could do it more regularly.

The important thing is that I've had some form of writing routine for the last ten years. That's added up to over a million words and a personal transformation I couldn't have dreamed of in a million years.

My writing routine continues to change depending on my work, time constraints, and goals. I'll go stretches of daily journaling, then months of journaling just once or twice. When I'm in the "messy middle" of a major project (a term coined by Scott Belsky), I'm constantly writing lists and notes for myself. When I'm in a more reflective mood, I enjoy writing exercises like freewriting and vision letters (more on those later). In my down time, I dabble in science fiction.

I will not try to prescribe a writing routine for you. It's one of those things that you need to figure out for yourself. But here's some advice for getting started:

Find the fastest path to writing. Get started as quickly as you can. Don't go searching for the perfect journal or the perfect time to write. Just write. It could be in an empty notebook, a sheet of paper, a Google Doc, your phone notes, or a journal with prompts. Experiment with different formats until you find one that feels easy for you.

Optimize for simplicity. You don't need a complex system to start writing. Just start somewhere—any-where—and build a system over time.

Collect ideas. Start a running list of writing ideas so that you always have something to dive into. I keep a list in Notion, but you can do this in your project management tool or even just your phone notes.

Block out writing time. Even if it's just fifteen minutes a day. If you try to write "when you have time," you'll never do it. Use your calendar to protect your writing time from work and other distractions.

Eliminate distractions. When writing, I hide my phone and use a website blocker that only gives me access to Google Docs. Fight the urge to check your email when you get stuck. If you don't know what to write, take a few deep breaths and then write whatever comes to mind next. I also highly recommend reading Nir Eyal's book *Indistractable* to learn how to fight distraction.

Set a timer. Setting a timer will help you stay focused on the task at hand. I became obsessed with using timers while writing this book. My writing sessions would be two or four blocks of fifty-three minutes with five minutes in between (Why fifty-three minutes? Fifty minutes felt too short and fifty-five minutes too intimidating. Fifty-three minutes just felt right.) My timer reminds me I don't need to write forever, but I do need to do it for the next sixteen minutes (or however long I have left). If you're new to using a timer, start with just twenty-five minutes. You'll be amazed how much writing you can get done in that time.

Set a ridiculously low goal for yourself. The first habit you must build is the habit of achievement. Set a writing goal so small that you can hit it no matter what. It could be writing for five minutes or writing one hundred words, or something even lower. The purpose is to build a writing streak. Once you start it, you won't want to stop. You'll begin to push yourself beyond your small goal to higher and higher achievements.

Hit publish. If you want to see exponential benefits from your writing, share it with the public. Hit send on a newsletter, blog post, or Twitter thread. You don't need to share everything you write, but sharing regularly will help you build an audience and solidify your ideas.

Wherever you are as a writer, just know this: If you're putting words on a page, that is enough. But if you want to improve the quality and quantity of your writing, next are several exercises for you to try.

13 WRITING EXERCISES FOR EVERY OCCASION

In this final chapter, I want to fill up your writing toolbox with some of my favorite exercises. There are tools for self-reflection, strategic planning, stress management, creativity, and more.

I've labeled each exercise with the following information:

✎ **Purpose:** For example, personal growth, strategic planning, or writing craft

⏱ **Time commitment:** How long each session should take

▲ **Difficulty:** How mentally or emotionally challenging the task is (Scale of 1–5)

Try out each exercise. Some you'll love, some you'll never do again. My simple hope is that they inspire you to write more.

The Bug Book

✎ Personal growth, self-reflection

◑ Less than 2 minutes

▲ 1 (easy)

Think back to when you were a kid. If you were anything like me, you were fascinated with bugs—at least the type with fewer than eight legs.

You'd be in the backyard and see an anthill in the grass or a cricket on the fence. You lean down to get a closer look. You'd noticed the cricket's legs, its eyes, and—*are those wings? I didn't know crickets had wings.* You'd watch the ants march dutifully in and out of their home. *Why are they doing that? Where are they going? What happens if I poke the anthill with a stick?*

Did you have any emotional attachment to these bugs while watching them? Probably not. You were just observing, like a biologist observes a specimen.

Self-improvement is difficult because we're emotionally attached to our own stories. It's hard to separate our actions from our motivations—our true feelings from our insecurities.

You've probably struggled with this. I certainly have.

To help me observe myself more objectively, I use a

writing exercise from legendary business writer Jim Collins, author of *Good to Great*.

He calls it "The Bug Book."

As a teenager, Collins struggled to find what he wanted to do in life. A teacher encouraged him to "study himself like a bug" and record his observations. The illusion helped Collins see himself from someone else's perspective—that of an indifferent researcher.

When I heard this story on *The Tim Ferriss Show* podcast, I immediately tried it out for myself. I used the bug book exercise to identify the type of work I enjoyed, activities that made me happy, and bad habits I needed to break.

I've created over one hundred observations in my bug book. Here are a few entries from over the years:

> "The bug Ben was extremely hungover on Sunday and didn't like it at all. He was also very embarrassed by being the most drunk person at the party. He's going to try avoiding that in the future."

> "The bug Ben really enjoyed presenting [to the Social Media Club of Kansas City] on Friday. He felt in his element up on stage, teaching people and making them laugh. It was stressful and nerve-wracking at first, but he knew his info and did really well."

> "When the bug doesn't get enough sleep, productivity becomes incredibly difficult. It's like pulling teeth. Every step is a drag. When the bug gets enough sleep, everything just flows. Sleep it big for the bug."

This exercise takes a little creativity. You must imagine

yourself as both the scientist and the specimen. Here are a few tips for getting started with your own bug book:

1. **Choose an on-the-go medium.** You don't have to use a physical journal for your bug book. I use the notes app on my phone and tag each entry with a label called "bug book." I prefer using my phone because I can take observations wherever I go.

2. **Be curious, but not judgmental.** Ask yourself, "Why did I do that?" or "Why do I feel this way?" not "Why am I so stupid?"

3. **Write in third person.** To stay judgment-free, refer to yourself in the third person. I go as far as to describe myself as "the bug Ben." This helps keep up the illusion of studying something other than myself.

4. **Be objective.** Observe your actions, emotions, and the connection between them, but don't try to assign a purpose or reason.

5. **Make daily observations.** Try to make at least one entry a day for one week. You'll be amazed by how much you learn.

The bug book is one of the most valuable personal development tools I've ever come across, and I still make entries to this day.

Get curious about yourself, like a child who studies a bug.

Reflection and Vision Letters

✎ Self-reflection, self-compassion, strategic planning

⏱ 30–60 minutes

⚠ 3 (Moderate)

Like the bug book, writing letters to yourself—past or present—is another way to look more objectively at your life.

For several years I've written a *vision story* to myself around New Year's. This is a letter I write to my *present* self from the perspective of myself one year into the future. This letter focuses on the year ahead (or the year past from the writer's perspective), what went well, what didn't go well, and important things I'll have learned. The vision letter can help you anticipate pitfalls and challenges before they happen.

But this year I added another letter to my year-end review. Commit Action, the productivity coaching service I've used since 2021, introduced me to the concept of a *reflection letter*. In this letter, your present self writes to your past self from one year ago. This letter is naturally more concrete than the vision letter because you're reflecting on the past, not imagining the future.

Writing this letter had a surprising impact on me. I was full of compassion for my past self—someone who had huge dreams but also massive insecurities. I got emotional when I told myself, "That goal you set of building a publishing business? *You fucking did it. You did it, dude.*"

In my opinion, there's no better way to build gratitude than writing to your past self. Because no matter how bad the past year was, there is one undeniable piece of good news: *You're still here.* And if you survived the past year, you have a chance to *thrive* this year.

Give the reflection letter and vision letter a try. Write to your past self and have your future self write to your present self.

Worry Lists

✎ Stress management

⏱ 10–15 minutes

⚠ 4 (challenging)

When I first started building Damn Gravity Media, I was drowning in worries.

There were big things like testing my business model, finding new authors, writing this book, and building my website. Then there were small things like registering my LLC, managing my existing content marketing clients, and building a budget. The tasks were never ending.

When anxiety took over, I found myself shutting down. My response to stress wasn't to fight or flee—it was to *freeze*. This made things worse. With a seemingly endless to-do list, doing *anything* would have been better than doing nothing.

In one particularly desperate moment of anxiety, I decided to try something different: I wrote down *everything* on my mind on a piece of paper—my work tasks, life worries, chores, random thoughts, and personal doubts. What happened next surprised even me: my anxiety melted away. I had control over the situation again. I knew what to do next and I got back to work.

This was how I developed one of my most important writing exercises: *the worry list*.

The worry list is exactly what it sounds like. It's a list of everything you're worried about personally, professionally, and otherwise. It includes your physical tasks like "edit blog post" and "clean the kitchen," but also your anxieties: "Am I being a good husband? Is my dog happy? Am *I* happy? Is my business going to fail?"

When your worries feel infinite, there's something deeply reassuring about writing them all down and getting to the end of the list. You realize that your problems are *finite*. There is, in fact, an end in sight.

Start by writing all your to-dos and worries in list form. I mean *everything*—leave nothing in your head. Then go back through your worry list and immediately cross off the ones that make no sense. *Am I being a good husband? Yes, we just had an amazing date night together.* Some things aren't actual problems, just projections of our self-doubt.

Then cross off the worries that are out of your control. You can't affect the stock market or how a potential client is going to respond to your proposal. You can only make wise financial decisions and put your best foot forward.

What's left on your list are tasks and problems that are in your control. Jot down an action item for each: What's the first step to solving this issue? You'll find that many of your worries are just a single step away from being solved. For everything else, block off the time on your calendar to complete it.

The worry list works because it takes your overwhelming problems and cuts them down to size: a single line on a piece of paper. If you find yourself frozen or spiraling from anxiety, write down everything on your mind. List out your worries so you can tackle them one-by-one.

Journaling

✏ Personal growth, self-reflection, gratitude, self-love, stress management

⏱ 5 – 10 minutes

▲ 2 (Easy)

Journaling is the simplest exercise to start building your writing routine. That's because there are basically no rules. Research has found that journaling is a powerful tool for dealing with stress, reflecting on past events, finding gratitude, and improving your confidence.

But many people let perfectionism hijack their journaling habit. They feel the need to journal every day, in the perfect notebook, with perfect thoughts. They have an all-or-nothing mentality when it comes to writing.

My wife, Mary, struggled with this for years. She didn't want to "mess up" her journals with writing she deemed not good enough. She didn't want to commit to a journaling routine because she didn't want the pressure of having to write every day. This led her to not writing at all.

But she eventually found a journaling routine that worked for her. First, she found a format that made it easy to get started. She always struggled with writing on a blank page, so she started using The Five-Minute Journal, which gives you the same writing prompts each day. Most importantly, Mary lowered her expectations. She doesn't write every day, and that's ok. She writes when she needs to.

It's one of life's most persistent and peculiar paradoxes: by letting go of expectations, you tend to exceed the ones you originally had in place.

There are countless ways to approach journaling. Personally, I enjoy just writing about my day and how I'm feeling. But sometimes it's useful to start with a few prompts. Here are twelve of my favorite:

1. **Gratitude**: What are three things I'm grateful for?
2. **Self-Love**: What are three things I love/appreciate about myself?
3. **Daily affirmation**: I am... [e.g., a writer, a badass founder]
4. **Values**: Today I want to be known as [list three to five values you care about; e.g., trustworthy]
5. **Goals**: What do I *really* want? Why?
6. **Productivity**: What is *one* thing I can do to make today feel like a success?
7. **Challenges**: What am I struggling with right now?
8. **Problem-Solving**: What would [person you admire] do in this situation?
9. **Reflection**: What are three amazing things that happened today/yesterday?
10. **Self-Improvement**: What would have made today/yesterday better?

11. **Wisdom**: What is in my control? What is not in my control?

12. **Self-Confidence:** What's something I did today that makes me really proud of myself?

To get started, choose a writing medium that's simple and accessible: either a notebook or even the notes app in your phone. Then set a goal to journal for five to ten minutes a day for one week.

Ecological Goal-Setting

✏ Strategic planning

⏱ 90–120 minutes

⚠ 5 (Difficult)

If you're an ambitious person (and if you're reading this book, my guess is you are), your goal-planning process probably looks like this:

1. Look at what your largest competitors are accomplishing.
2. Set a large, number-based goal with an aggressive timeline (e.g., $10 million in revenue in six months).
3. Write it down in a notebook or on a white board.
4. Forget about it.

When setting goals for our businesses or personal lives, we tend to pull big numbers out of thin air. I know I've done this dozens of times. These goals are exciting, but have little or no grounding in reality. The only thing these types of goals do is set you up for disappointment.

Don't get me wrong: big, aggressive goals are great. But if you don't have a plan to achieve them, they aren't goals at all—they're dreams (or worse, delusions).

To set the right goals for your business, use a technique called *ecological goal-setting*. This is an exercise I learned from Peter Shallard, a business psychologist and founder of Commit Action, a coaching service for entrepreneurs.

Start by setting a BHAG: a big, hairy, audacious goal. Then ask yourself these twelve questions to get clear on *why* you want to achieve that goal and *how* you'll get it done:

1. What, specifically, do you want? Consider what your ideal future looks like: What you're doing, with whom, and the impact you're making.
2. Where are you now in terms of achieving this goal?
3. What will you see, hear, and feel when you succeed? Try to imagine this moment as vividly as possible.
4. How will you know when you achieved it? What evidence do you need?
5. What will this outcome get for you or allow you to do?
6. Is it 100 percent self-initiated and self-maintained? Is any part of this goal out of your control? (Or in the words of Naval Ravikant, is it permissionless?)

7. When, where, and with whom do you want to achieve this goal?
8. What resources are needed?
9. *Why* do you want this? Ask yourself this question three to five times to get to your core motivation.
10. What will you gain or lose if you achieve it?
11. What will happen if you achieve this goal? What *won't* happen if you get it?
12. What will happen if I *don't* achieve this goal? What *won't* happen if I don't get it?

Take your time answering these twelve questions. They will save you months of wasted effort by ensuring your goals actually make sense in the grand scheme of things.

After Action Review

✒ Strategic planning, self-improvement, team-improvement

⏱ 30–45 minutes

⚠ 3 (moderate)

When building a business, lessons will be repeated until they are learned. The best organizations don't just reflect on the past—they use a deliberate system to capture those learnings and implement them.

The After Action Review (AAR) is a tool developed by the U.S. military to debrief and learn from past missions, successful or failed. After a mission, the team recaps by asking four questions:

- What was supposed to happen? (mission and intent)
- What did happen? (results)
- What went well?
- Where can we improve?

In my opinion, a project isn't over until you conduct an AAR. Otherwise you risk letting valuable lessons go to waste. Spend time with your team to review every project, event, launch, and campaign. Make sure to capture improvements in a place where you'll see and implement them for the next project.

You can also do AARs for yourself. For example, I'll conduct an AAR at the end of a difficult week. Not only does this help me capture important lessons, but it reminds me of what I did well that week. AARs give you an objective, balanced perspective on your past performance, and most importantly, insights on what you can do better next time.

Pre-Mortem Planning

✏ Strategic planning

⏱ 30 minutes

⚠ 3 (moderate)

Some people resist the urge to think about the worst-case scenario. But if you're really committed to achieving big things, you need to think about what could go wrong.

The *pre-mortem* is an exercise developed by psychologist Gary Klein. Unlike an After Action Review, a pre-mortem is conducted *before* embarking on a new project or path. Your goal is to visualize the failure of your endeavor and figure out how to avoid it.

It starts like this:

Imagine it's the day after the big launch and it was an unmitigated FAILURE. How did things go so wrong?

Answer this question in as much detail as possible. By projecting yourself into the future, you'll see pitfalls you didn't consider before. For example, you may envision that no news outlets picked up the story, or your brand partners weren't as committed as you expected. Maybe your team didn't know their roles on the day of the launch.

Andy Ellwood takes the pre-mortem one step further. At a recent offsite with his startup team, he asked these four questions during the exercise:

- Final moments: What happened moments before it was over?
- Time of death: When would you know it wasn't working?
- Cause of death: What was the fatal blow?
- Final wishes: What will you have wished you had done?

These questions make the pre-mortem even more real and concrete. "I have never seen more clarity and urgency," Ellwood said. "The team is ready to run through walls together."

The more detailed you can be in your pre-mortem, the

better prepared you'll be for the unexpected. Add details big and small to put yourself in the shoes of your future self. Feel the emotion of the situation. Then work backwards to determine how to win and avoid disaster.

Decision Review

✏️ Decision-making

⏱️ 5–10 minutes

⚠️ 2 (Easy)

There are several variations of the After Action Review. One of my favorites is something I call a *decision review*. Instead of focusing on outcomes, as the AAR does, a decision review focuses squarely on your decision-making, regardless of the outcome.

In her book *Thinking in Bets*, psychology professor and professional poker player Annie Duke argues that your decisions should be evaluated separately from your results. In poker, as in the real world, there is a lot we can't control that affects the outcome. The best we can do is try to make better decisions.

At the end of the week, month, or quarter, ask yourself three simple questions:

- What good decisions did I make? Why were they good?
- What poor decisions did I make? Why were they bad?
- Where can I improve my decision-making tomorrow?

If you find these questions useful, take it a step further with decision journaling.

Decision Journaling

✏ Decision-making

⏱ 10–15 minutes

⚠ 3 (moderate)

Decision reviews are useful, but it's hard to be objective when evaluating a decision after the fact. Hindsight bias can creep into your analysis and alter your view. The best way to improve your decisions is by evaluating them before *and* after you get the result.

Decision journaling is simple: whenever you make a major decision, write it down in a journal or note. Explain *why* you made the decision and a hypothesis about the result. Be as specific as possible. Then add a reminder in your calendar to review your decision after the result.

The concept of decision journaling comes from the world of stock trading. Traders often use a tool called an *investment journal* to record their trades, their reasoning behind it, and a hypothesis for the outcome. After the trade is complete, traders have an objective record of whether their strategy was right or wrong.

Decision journaling gives you the most objective view of your decision-making process. It allows you to separate good decisions from bad outcomes, and most deceptively, bad luck.

For example, say you decide to partner with another

business in your industry on a joint marketing campaign. They have a larger audience than you, and you have a skill set they need to take full advantage of it. Your hypothesis: $100,000 in revenue in six months.

But after six months, you've only made $25,000 together. What happened?

It turns out their audience was large but mostly unengaged. You made the right decision to partner with a larger company, but you chose the wrong partner. In the future, you'll evaluate a partner's engagement metrics before agreeing to a joint campaign.

Try decision journaling for yourself. Next time you make a big decision, write it down. Record your reasoning and a hypothesis for the outcome, then set a reminder in your calendar to review. Did the decision turn out how you expected? If not, what happened? And what can you improve for next time?

PR/FAQ

✎ Strategic planning, new product launch

⏱ 5–10 hours

⚠ 5 (Difficult)

Amazon is one of the most innovative companies in history. They've revolutionized dozens of industries, including retail, cloud computing, logistics, publishing, smart speakers, and more.

One of Amazon's secret weapons is the way they communicate within the company. Most organizations rely on PowerPoints and spreadsheets to present new ideas.

But at Amazon, PowerPoint slides are banned and replaced by six-page written narratives. The first twenty minutes of every meeting are eerily quiet as everyone reads the narrative from the product lead.

The PR/FAQ is a style of narrative developed specifically for new product development. Two long-time Amazon executives, Colin Bryar and Bill Carr, cover the process in detail in their excellent book, *Working Backwards: Insights, Stories, and Secrets from Inside Amazon.*

"Written narratives will convey your ideas in a deeper, stronger, more capable fashion while adding a key additional benefit: they will act as a forcing function that shapes sharper, more complete analysis," said the authors.

The PR/FAQ is a tool every founder should use when considering a new product or service to deliver. It shifts the conversation from, "What's good for the company?" to "What's good for our customers?" It's fundamentally an exercise in empathy.

The PR/FAQ is split into two sections: the press release (PR) and the frequently asked questions (FAQ).

A press release is something typically released at the end of product development and right before launch. Instead, Amazon flips the conventional model on its head. Product owners write the press release at the very beginning of the development process. This is how they introduce the project to the rest of the team. It forces the product owner to think through the most important question: "Why should the customer care?"

A standard press release has seven sections and is no more than a page long:

- **Title**: Announcement of new product or service

- **Sub-title**: One-sentence "pitch" for customers
- **Summary paragraph**: Sharing details such as what the product does, why it was developed, and how much it will cost.
- **Problem paragraph**: Explain the challenges customers face that led to the development of the product. The "old" status quo.
- **Solution paragraph**: Highlight the most valuable features of the product or service that solves the customer's problems.
- **Testimonial**: Share quotes from customers (in this case, fake customers) explaining why they chose the new product/service
- **Next steps**: When, where, and how customers can purchase the new product or service.

Following the press release is the FAQ section. Here is where the product owner must consider and answer the hardest questions they can think of. The FAQ section is typically split into an external FAQ (questions from customers) and internal FAQ (questions from team and company leaders). Amazonians try to keep the FAQ section to five pages.

Creating a good PR/FAQ is much harder than putting together a slide deck, and that's the point. It forces product owners to think deeply about the product or service from the customer's point of view. It's not uncommon for PR/FAQs to go through ten-plus revisions at Amazon.

In the earliest stages of product development, the only question that really matters is, "Why should the customer care?" If the product isn't better in some way—either faster, more convenient, higher quality, or improves the experience—then all the other details don't matter. The PR/FAQ will help you filter product and service ideas through this crucial question.

We can all learn from Amazon's use of written narratives to drive innovation. It forces deep, clear, and concise thinking while giving your team the information they need to make good decisions quickly.

Copywork

✎ Copywriting, writing style

⏱ 10–20 minutes

⚠ 3 (moderate)

You know good writing when you see it. But producing good writing is an entirely different skill set.

It's like seeing a slick crossover move on the basketball court—you can't just watch it and recreate the move yourself. You must practice. And practice. And practice until your arms fall off. You won't be able to do the move until you develop the right technique and muscle memory.

As a kid in school, you were probably tasked to copy excerpts from a book. This wasn't just busy work. It's called *copywork*, and it's one of the best ways to improve your writing.

Copywork is simply the act of rewriting a piece of writing you enjoy. The goal is to reproduce an exact copy of the original work: word for word, comma for comma. This process helps you develop the muscle memory to create great writing yourself. (I shouldn't have to say this, but here's your reminder to *not* plagiarize other people's writing by passing it off as your own. This is just a writing exercise.)

You can use copywork to improve all forms of writing. If you're working on your copywriting skills, copy the top-selling ads and sales emails. If better storytelling is your goal, rewrite your favorite short story or essay. If you want to learn how to write books, *rewrite your favorite books.*

Copywork is not a new idea. You might recognize it from the introduction of this book: Benjamin Franklin used a variation of copywork in his self-taught writing lessons.

If you want to become a better writer, start by copying the greats.

Freewriting

✏ Creativity, stress management

⏱ 5–15 minutes

⚠ 3 (Moderate)

Freewriting is one of the best tools to unleashing your creativity.

I was first inspired to try freewriting by Natalie Goldberg, a writing teacher and author of several writing books, including *Writing Down the Bones.* She showed me the power of freewriting to knock down mental barriers and let your wildest thoughts flow like water through a broken dam.

This exercise is simple: Set a timer for fifteen minutes. Then start writing and don't stop for *anything*. Don't let your pen or fingers stop moving until the timer goes off. Write down whatever comes to mind, even if it's gibberish. Let your brain go to places it's never gone before. Let your fingers develop words they've never ventured to make.

Freewriting is more than just a tool for creativity. It will also help you defeat the perfectionist streak that holds you back. It teaches you to break through writer's block—not with a scalpel, but a sledgehammer. If you find yourself staring at a blank page, set a timer and freewrite until you find the right words to start your work.

If you're new to freewriting, fifteen minutes will feel like an eternity. If that's the case, try to do it for ten minutes. Too long? Try five minutes. Still hard? Set a timer for just one minute.

Freewriting will set your mind on fire with ideas. It will break you free from the shackles of self-doubt, fuzzy thinking, and high expectations. For many people, freewriting feels like finding your voice for the first time.

40-Minute Fiction

✎ Creativity

⏱ 40 minutes

⚠ 4 (Challenging)

What type of story would you tell if it didn't have to be rooted in reality? Now is your chance to find out just how far your imagination can go. Even for non-fiction writers, writing fiction is a brilliant way to boost your creativity. It will make you feel alive with ideas and excitement.

If you've never written fiction, where should you start? I recommend an exercise I did frequently in middle school. The state of Ohio has a program called Power of the Pen, a state-wide creative writing competition. Each middle school has a team that competes at district, regional, and state-level tournaments.

The main event at these writing tournaments is the forty-minute fiction round.

Set a timer for forty minutes, then use a random writing prompt generator to give yourself a prompt (search online for "random writing prompt generator"). Use your forty minutes to write a short story based on that prompt.

If you're struggling to get started, remember this: all fiction is rooted in reality. Even galactic sci-fi books reflect our human nature in some way. Don't search too far outside yourself to find inspiration. Write what you know.

The benefit of the forty-minute timer is that it keeps you focused on writing and not thinking. This is the entire point. This exercise will unleash a typhoon of creative energy within you.

MASTER THE CRAFT AND THE TOOL

No matter what writing exercises you use, writing for yourself is one of the most powerful habits an entrepreneur can build.

Writing for yourself helps clarify your thinking, improve your judgment, flex your creative muscles, and build empathy. Writing is also a way to vent. When things are going wrong—when you're overwhelmed by the stresses of building a company—writing is both cathartic and productive. That's a rare combination.

Incorporate writing into your daily life with these exercises. Try them all to see which ones work best for you. Once one exercise becomes a habit, add another. And don't forget to enjoy every minute of it.

As a founder, you write for your audiences, customers, teammates, and investors. But at the end of the day, the most important person to write for is yourself.

FREE TOOL #8 BONUS:
Writing Exercises and Templates

Want to start writing, but don't know where do start? It's easier when you have an exercise regimen.

Go to **www.greatfounderswrite.com/bonus**, enter your email, then click on "Writing Exercises and Templates" to get the free tools. These templates will help you start writing in just three clicks of the mouse.

POSTSCRIPT:
THE WORK HAS JUST BEGUN

"You don't start out writing good stuff. You start out writing crap and thinking it's good stuff, and then gradually you get better at it. That's why I say one of the most valuable traits is persistence."

—OCTAVIA E. BUTLER

This book has shown you the principles, frameworks, and tools to become a great founder through the power of writing. Now comes the hard part: turning your words into action.

Benjamin Franklin is considered one of the greatest writers in American history, but he was a *doer* first and foremost. He didn't just write about his disagreements with the governing Penn family of Pennsylvania—he actively defied them and their corrupt policies. He built coalitions, proposed new laws, and spent decades in London lobbying the British Parliament. When King George III failed to support the American cause, Franklin didn't just write about the injustices of the crown—he took up arms against them.

When Arlan Hamilton saw the lack of venture capital funding for underrepresented founders, she didn't just write a scathing viral blog post about it (which she did). She founded her own venture firm: Backstage Capital, the name an homage to her days as a touring band manager. Backstage Capital has since invested in over two hundred companies led by underrepresented founders.

Keith Gill, a family man known as Roaring Kitty and DFV among online traders, didn't just write a compelling thesis on why GameStop was undervalued—he invested $53,000 of his own savings into the stock, thus kickstarting the historic short squeeze in January 2021. The bet made him a multimillionaire and icon. At the same time, Public.com didn't just courageously speak up for retail traders during the GameStop stock freeze. Just days after the incident, the trading platform announced they would no longer accept Payment for Order Flow, the controversial practice that made up a majority of rival Robinhood's revenue. The decision would better align the startup with their mission of empowering *all* investors, not just the financial elite.

Clear thinking leads to confident writing. Confident writing leads to decisive action.

All the PR/FAQs in the world mean nothing if Amazon doesn't take the best ideas and execute on them. You can create the perfect Heroic Customer Story and ABC123 copywriting framework, but they won't matter if you don't do the work to promote your startup.

Great founders don't just write—they take the *right* action:

- They start with the end in mind.
- They build empathy with their customers.

- They communicate clearly and intentionally.
- They lead and write with courage, even when it's hard.

And that's just the beginning. As you've seen throughout this book, writing will help you improve every part of your business, from strategic planning to training employees. Make writing the basis of your company culture and watch the benefits compound over time.

Perhaps the greatest benefit of writing, though, is the confidence you'll gain in yourself. I hope you join the ranks of entrepreneurs and great leaders through the ages who have used writing as the catalyst for personal transformation. Because when your thoughts become words on a page, they can suddenly be questioned, critiqued, and refined. It's quite literally like writing your ideal life into existence.

Beyond that, I hope the stories, frameworks, writing prompts, and exercises in this book help you become a better founder. I wrote *Great Founders Write* to be a resource—something to be read slowly and repeatedly as you put the teachings into practice. Use these ideas to create your own writing routine and develop exercises that work for *you*.

Finally, I hope this book has sparked or rekindled your love of writing—not just as a tool, but also a source of joy, comfort, and creativity. I hope it gives you the courage to be relentless as a founder, creator, and person.

Since the days of Kushim in the ancient city of Ur, entrepreneurs have used writing to propel the world forward.

Now it's your turn to create something worth writing about.

ACKNOWLEDGMENTS

Wow, where to begin.

I've wanted to write a book for as long as I can remember, so I'll start by thanking Mom, Dad and my stepmom, Deb for encouraging my early interest in writing. You bought me my first books, drove me to and from writing competitions, and supported me through years of school. When I decided to become an entrepreneur and author, you encouraged me every step of the way. I love you all. Thank you for this life you gave me.

I also want to thank my sister Julianne, a fellow entrepreneur and my writing muse. You inspire me with your energy, wisdom, and strength. Thank you to my older sister, Kristi, who was the first writer and author I knew, and my brother, CJ, whose passion for life brings me joy every day. And a big thank you to Uncle Jeff, who sparked my curiosity for learning at a young age. Love y'all.

This book was far from a solo effort. I would have never finished it without my productivity coach, Victoria Lopez. You helped me stay motivated and on track for eighteen whole months. Can't thank you enough.

From the beginning I committed to writing it in public. Thank you to all my friends and colleagues who have given me feedback during the process. A special thank you to Kjell Vandevyvere, who not only edited my book but gave me the kick in the butt to finally publish it. I also want to thank my beta readers who spent their precious time reading a sub-par version of this book: Max Curatella, Margaret Ryland, Colleen Sheehan, John Paul Hernandez, Andrew Yang, Sara Feldstein, Jess Rohloff, and my good friend Chris Piggott, who, along with Julianne, was the person I wrote this book for.

Next, I want to thank some of my oldest friends: Kyle Bayes, Ryan Clair, and Amish Patel. You guys have supported my wild dreams every step of the way. I wouldn't be the man I am today without you guys. Love y'all.

Finally, I want to thank my wife, Mary. You have been by my side since the beginning of this grueling journey called entrepreneurship. You've seen me at my lowest and highest moments, always supportive and reminding me of what's important. You have been my rock and best friend every step of the way. I don't know what I did to get so lucky. Everything I do, I do for you. I love you.

Thank you all. Here's to the next one!

ABOUT THE
AUTHOR

B en Putano is a writer, entrepreneur, and book publisher. He's the founder of Damn Gravity Media, a publishing house that inspires and educates tomorrow's great founders. Ben lives in Chicago with his wife, Mary, and is an avid ultimate frisbee player.

Connect with Ben on Twitter:
www.twitter.com/BenjaminPutano

Made in the USA
Monee, IL
20 November 2022

18202916R10125